Miles

From

Nowhere

Miles

From

Nowhere

An Inevitable Journey of Love and Self-Discovery

Victoria Takács

Victoria Takács
12 Village Rd., Unit 170
New Vernon, New Jersey 07976
www.victoriatakacs.com
www.victoriatakacs.com/contactus/
www.facebook.com/MilesFromNowhereBook/
email: VictoriaTakacsAuthor@gmail.com
email: VictoriaTakacsMeditation@gmail.com

ISBN-13: 978-0-9979875-0-8

Photographs by
José Domingo Herrera (cover image)
&
Catherine Leonard Photography (photo of author)

Editted by
Dru Reed Mogge & Sharon Laverty Gallagher

Printed in the United States of America

This book is lovingly dedicated to Elizabeth Chadbourne DuBois (Namu), who showed me how to *live* with my whole heart.

"Miles From Nowhere"

Miles from nowhere, guess I'll take my time, oh yeah, to reach there.

Look up at the mountain I have to climb, oh yeah, to reach there.

Lord my body has been a good friend, but I won't need it when I reach the end.

Miles from nowhere, guess I'll take my time. O yeah, to reach there. Oh yeah.

I creep through the valleys and I grope through the woods, cause I know when I find my honey

It's gonna make me feel good, yes.

I love everything, so don't it make it make you feel sad,

'Cause I'll drink to you, my baby, I'll think to that, I'll think to that.

Miles from nowhere, not a soul in sight, oh yeah, but it's alright.

I have my freedom, I can make my own rules, oh yeah, the ones that I choose.

Lord my body has been a good friend, but I won't need it when I reach the end.

I love everything, so don't it make you feel sad, 'cause I'll drink to you my baby,

I'll think to that, yes, I'll think to that. Think to that, oh yeah.

Miles from nowhere, guess I'll take my time, oh yeah, to reach there.

Songwriter: Cat Stevens

Contents

Preface xi
Acknowldgements xv
Introduction xix

1. Sanctuary 1
2. Uprooted 5
3. Saturday Night Fever, The Extended Version . . . 19
4. Bright Lights, Hot Nights 25
5. Mount Olympus 31
6. "An Act Of God" 39
7. Modern-Day Pioneers 49
8. The Jersey Shore 59
9. Doctor Richards 65
10. Refuge 75
11. "Back To School" 79
12. Ethics 85
13. "KHS" 89
14. The Rock of Gibralter 99
15. Early Retirement 111
16. Home of My Ancestors 119

Epilogue 129
About the Author 135

PREFACE

S uch was the determination of my soul to be brought into this world that destinies from opposite corners of the globe would have to collide, against all odds and reason, to bring me here, to this life.

Zsolt Takács was born into an upper-class family in Budapest, Hungary, during the early years of WWII. His father was a physician whose medical competence, wisdom, and charitable nature had made him an adored and revered member of society. His mother, born into Transylvanian aristocracy, was a stunning, intelligent woman with a warrior spirit, who raised her six children with tough love.

Soon after, on the other side of the world, squarely in the heart of America's mid-west, Nancy Mills was born in St. Louis, Missouri. Her parents were devout Christian Scientists, as was her mother's entire family. She was an only child. Her parents' marriage ended when Nancy was around thirteen. Shortly thereafter, she transitioned from being a day student to a resident at Principia, a private boarding school and, according to my mother, the center of the social scene in St. Louis. Luckily, she loved it.

The Hungarian Revolution of 1956 began as a spontaneous revolt resulting from policies having been imposed on the Hungarian People's Republic by the Soviet Union. Russian troops occupied Budapest and took possession of my father's (circa 1500) manor, leaving the family immediately homeless. My grandfather was incarcerated because of his strong political influence. At seventeen, my father and a friend escaped, on foot, unknowingly criss-crossing frozen, live minefields three times, until they reached Moschendorf, Austria, at which time they were immediately shipped to a refugee camp. Their flight took many life-threatening turns before they reached safety. (The details of my father's life, including his miraculous survival during this harrowing escape, merit a book of its own, which I hope to write one day.) Zsolt Takács astonishingly landed on his feet, alive and kicking, in Brattleboro, Vermont, at the Experiment of International Living (EIL). One of the first people my father met was devoted secretary and staunch supporter of the EIL mission, none other than my grandmother, Elizabeth DuBois.

EIL was and is a foreign exchange organization, placing American students with families abroad and vice versa. The end goal is brilliant and simple: by offering the experience of living how others live, compassion and understanding are naturally cultivated, thereby encouraging international peace.

At the time my dad had fallen into the loving arms of EIL, an extraordinary and singular twist of fate materialized: ten local families came forward and specifically solicited Hungarian refugees to sponsor. As these adolescents were neither "exchange students" nor returning to their mother country, an unusual circumstance presented itself to the EIL and a fortuitous opportunity materialized for my father. He was soon placed with a caring family who would teach him English and help him to graduate high school. Ultimately, he was accepted into three highly regarded universities. This however, would not transpire until the end of the summer of '57.

To tie this fairy tale up with a beautiful bow, my mom spent her summer vacations from boarding school in Vermont with her mother. In the magical summer of 1957, Divine will intervened and Zsolt and Nancy met. It was, as they say, love at first sight, in every sense of the word. It wouldn't be long before I came along. Both my parents have independently told me, "No child has ever been more loved and wanted than you were." Being born as the result of pure love gives a person's soul an extra dose of fortitude that never fades. As if giving me life weren't enough, this is the cherry on top for which I will be eternally thankful.

Acknowledgments

I would like to express my humble gratitude to my parents, Nancy Chadbourne Mills and Zsolt Bence Takács, who brought me into this world, with courageous love. They each gave their part in making me the warrior I am.

I wish to honor and declare my unfathomable respect for my daughters, Stefani and Elizabeth, who chose me. They are unquestionably my greatest teachers and most treasured companions.

I would like to acknowledge my sister, Kathryn Íldiko Takács Taylor, and my brother, Paul Thomas Takács, who each in their own way have been lion-hearted representations of tenacity and love.

I celebrate the existence of Juan Pablo Flores Guerrero, from whom I have learned by example: patience, love, and the grace of letting go. He is an exceptional human being who has helped me to better understand and respect the male species.

I would like to extend my boundless appreciation to Sharon Laverty Gallagher, cherished friend, editor, and believer, without whom (much more than) this book would not have been possible.

I would like to affirm my sincere affection and esteem for Dru Reed Mogge, one of few in this world who truly know and understand me, and whose unwavering friendship and support have helped me through the darkest of times.

I would also like to recognize the contribution of the numerous people who have touched my life and given generously of their time, their love, and their resources to support me on my journey. A partial list includes: Shivagam, Maha Vajra, Lourdes Aguirre Martínez, Erika Graiff, Guru Citta (Iliana Zeferin), Lakshmi Shakti (Diana Turner), Ganesh Ananda (Sujey Rodríguez), Leticia Roel Barrantes, Gaby Zermeño, Androna Elias Calles, Oyuz Iyari Agni Hrdaya (Rosalba Gómez), Suzann Brucato, Shanti Lesur, Eduardo Cruz, Christian Valeriani, Dick Muise, Juan Fenton Brown, Francisca Altamirano Celis, Silvia Guerrero Castillo, Emmanuel Flores Guerrero, Luis Felipe Flores Guerrero, Maria Larreddola Takács, Chalmer Taylor, Pamela Furlong, Ruth Palacio, Daree Rose, Madison Orlando, Grace Lang, Kevin Murphy, Salvatore Dispenziere III, Jeanie Cronin Coomber, Eric Sauer, Francisco

Santos Carbajhal, Janet Sullivan Watson, Paula Phillips, and Jennifer Corey.

Introduction

I lie in Savasana, eyes closed. I am completely relaxed except for my conscious willingness to receive thoughts. Lately, some of my best ideas have appeared, seemingly out of the blue, just like this. I have recently discovered these are much more than thoughts.

When I was young and forced to go to Sunday school, the Bible talked about "God speaking to every-body." I imagined it as some kind of ominous, dramatic occurrence, like a scene from the epic 1956 film, *The Ten Commandments*.

The benefits of prayer and meditation are subtle. They creep into your life little by little, until one day you notice things have shifted. You feel more peaceful for sure, but there are other wonderful byproducts as well: heightened intuition, good ideas, and enhanced creativity, to name a few. It's like when you've had chronic pain for a long time and finally make a decision to do something about it. You have become so accustomed to living with the discomfort that it takes a while to notice its absence. Then once you do, it feels like floating down a stream on a sunny day. Sublime.

The idea for this book came to me at the end of a yoga class. It sounded like a command in my head, "Write a book!" That's it. I went home and immediately began to write. This book wanted to be born. I must have been carrying it around inside of me for a long time because it flowed onto the pages in an effortless birth.

This narrative is my heartfelt gift to anyone who may discover it by chance or by design. Om Shanti.

1

Sanctuary

Present day, 2017, Cuernavaca, Morelos, Mexico

"There, but for the grace of God, go I."
—John Bradford [attributed]

The spirited chirp of many birds awakens me. Daylight has not yet broken but there are hungry mouths to feed; several sparrows have made their home beneath the clay-tiled roof of my condominium and, by the sound of things, there are recent additions to their families. It's a little before 6 a.m. so I have enough time to wake up in a leisurely manner before yoga class at 8:20. I rise from my delicious bed and walk through the dark to the living room, light three white candles, wrap myself in a cozy Indian blanket, and settle into my morning meditation. It is my absolute favorite time of the day. I am enveloped in comfort and quiet. The windows are open, as they almost always are, but there is a clean crispness in the mountain air that will soon be replaced by the customarily sunny, temperate weather Cuernavaca is known for. I love breathing in chilly air while the rest of my body is cocooned in warmth. I allow thoughts to float in and out of my mind like clouds coming and going on a breezy day. I alternate between gazing at the flickering candles and closing my eyes while pondering the ever-growing list of things I am grateful for. This portion of my daily meditations takes about an hour, after which I prepare one of the elements from my "gratitude list": a big pot of coffee. My daily cup of freshly ground and brewed java is an early morning gift of the gods.

I return to my living room, speckled with the first glimmers of morning sun. It's the perfect place to enjoy my coffee. Now visible are the simple yet rustically elegant and comfortable surroundings. At the center of this space, inside my moderately-sized residence, is a trickling fountain that empties into a six by six-foot koi pond, tucked inside lush vegetation, flowers, and small palm trees. This is the heart of my home. "How fortunate I am," I note for the third or fourth time since I've awakened, "to be living in this not-so-small town nestled in the mountains of central Mexico, where the year-round climate together with abundant, exotic foliage are responsible for its moniker, 'The Land of Eternal Spring'!"

The serenity, peace, and slow pace I have craved most of my adult life are at last a reality. My days vary but almost always consist of the following components: the aforementioned meditation and coffee ritual; savoring the magnificent postcard vista of a distant, live volcano framed by my bedroom window; and writing in my journal.

Most days I practice yoga. On the days I don't, I go for a swim in the crystalline (almost always vacant) swimming pool that belongs to my small condominium complex. My breakfast is a huge green shake with protein powder and whatever six to eight fresh vegetables I have on hand. The rest of my day mostly consists of teaching (private or group) guided-meditation classes, both locally and internationally (via SKYPE), low-key encounters with friends, spiritual studies, attending workshops or retreats, and currently, working on this book.

Perhaps this outline does not appeal to the reader as book-worthy. I am, after all, describing my life now: an ultra tranquil, not terribly exciting existence, the design for which I have spent decades searching. . . The bigger picture however, consists of a lifetime of adventures, life-threatening scenarios, fear, uncertainty, and confusion, woven into a fabric of dauntless determination. My quest to find answers to the unidentifiable questions that had been haunting me since adolescence was spurred by an ongoing, nagging feeling that something wasn't right, that I somehow was not being true to myself.

This is quite a unique story. The old adage, "fact is stranger than fiction", is one I have found to be true about many people's lives. Upon reflection, I discover that mine seems to have had some particularly interesting and sharp turns. It's been a magical trip, for sure, though not entirely fun. Still, the cast of characters and chains of events found herein could not have been avoided nor programmed, even had I wanted to. The Universe had its own plan.

2

Uprooted

Summer 1975, Toms River, New Jersey

My mom and stepfather got married in mid-December and left immediately for a weeklong honeymoon on Harbour Island, Bahamas. We (my sister, brother, and I), like most products of divorce, were not overjoyed with the idea of my mom re-marrying. Looking back though, I personally didn't expend much energy toward the emotion of unhappiness (at least not outwardly). Actually, this moment may be better marked as the embryonic phase of a "suspended animation" that spanned more than half my lifetime. This era was defined by the extensive use of mind-numbing agents, along with other varied forms of distraction, such as thrill seeking and frenzied behavior. It continued to escalate over the years until the tipping point was reached, around age fifty-five.

Each of my siblings and I had attended Wilmington Friends School in Wilmington, Delaware, since kindergarten. My mother had somehow arranged for us to be awarded scholarships (without which we could have never afforded the lofty tuition). This alone was a testament of her devotion to us and her awareness of the importance of an outstanding education. WFS is a small, private Quaker school known for its pedagogically superior level of instruction. Its academic rigor is on par with its ethics, which mirror the founders' impeccable moral code. It is an exemplary institution, and we were beyond fortunate to be there.

This information is relevant because a day or two after the newlyweds had left for their trip, I was caught drinking in the parking lot at a school dance. I was fifteen. This type of comportment was quite uncommon, almost unheard of at our school. The Administration was stunned by my behavior. I had never had a disciplinary issue at school. I was a good, rule-abiding, and borderline shy kid. I was given "in-school suspension" for the entire week before Christmas. I wasn't privy to the conversations that ensued between my mom and the headmaster when she returned from her trip, but I'm sure they considered this an act of rebellion against her new marriage. It was only the beginning.

When June rolled around, we found out we were leaving the town where I grew up. We were migrating, about an hour and a half away, from Delaware to Central Jersey. My mother, bless her warrior spirit, vowed that we would continue to commute from our new home to Wilmington Friends School, so as not to interfere with the constant that had been in our lives since kindergarten. Since I had quickly become involved with a new boyfriend, and his circle of high school buddies as soon as we got to New Jersey, I nixed my mom's proposition. There was no way I would waste eleven hours of my time everyday, when I could enroll in the local public high school and be close to my newfound friends. I also had high aspirations of joining the gymnastic team, which would take the sting out of abandoning the team of which I had been part since early childhood. This was probably the only reason I was able to convince my mother to let me have my way. Nevertheless (and true to form), she held up her end of the bargain with my sister and brother, but it proved to be too much for all concerned, and the well-intended, daily excursion lasted only for the first year.

One of several things that most impacted me about moving away was leaving my gymnastic team, Olympiad Gymnastics. I originally joined this club because at the age of eight (according to my grandmother), I was enrolled in after-school classes for the sole purpose of expending my seemingly never-ending supply of energy. The twice-a-week, unstructured tumbling classes gradually became more methodized daily sessions, Monday through Friday. By the time I reached seventh grade, I was moved to a junior team, most of whose participants were being groomed for the elite traveling team. I began competing on a novice level, but by ninth grade I had become proficient enough to be asked to join a nationally sanctioned team. In an instant, practices became a major part of my life, with four-hour plus practices on both Saturdays and Sundays, in addition to daily weeknight training sessions. The standards were rigorous, to say the least. We trained year around, with intense, month-long camp immersions over the summers. It was not out of the realm of possibility for one or more members of the elite team to reach near Olympic status, qualifying for try-outs on more than one occasion during my tenure with the team. The requirements and demands of our coaching staff were far beyond what one might consider "acceptable" from those whose sights were

set on international recognition and glory. The atmo-
sphere was borderline abusive. There were stringent
weight restrictions that required weekly weigh-ins.
Our "competition weight" was well below average
health standards. If we failed to pass our personal
weight limit at any given time, we were sidelined
from the next competition. Bulimia, laxatives, and
diuretics were all standard practice for many members on the team. I remember being taught how to
provoke vomiting at summer camp when I was thirteen. This became a practice that transformed into
a serious illness that haunted me and jeopardized
my health for more than thirty years.

Long-term mentor/teacher relationships with
protégés/students can become psychologically
dysfunctional, especially if the arena in which the
mentor and student operate is isolated from the rest
of the world. Further, if this encompasses the span
of a student's formative, impressionable years, it
can rob the child of crucial social communion with
peers, not unlike being home-schooled or being a
child actor. My gymnastic club was, in large part, all
I knew. It was my "family." Although I had also participated in interscholastic sports at school, to some
extent I had become insulated, having had limited
social exposure and interaction. In terms of being
rescued from the dark underbelly of the gymnastic

world, moving to New Jersey was probably a godsend; but at the time, I would have done anything to remain with my captor, so to speak.

The perfect storm of uncertainty in my life (my parents' divorce, followed by moving out of town) presented a precarious foundation from which to make a successful transition to my new life. I was perfectly primed to morph into someone who was desperate to belong and impress. I had unwittingly transformed into a person who was willing to exchange my autonomy for acceptance; it was right out of the textbooks; every parent's nightmare.

As humans, it is our nature to resist change. We are comfortable with what we know, whether positive or negative; that which is familiar seems easier. Our natural, initial reaction to instability, anger, or shame is often rebellion or denial. I experienced both. As a matter of fact, at the time I was incapable of embracing "the change" as a valuable lesson. Instead, I assumed a character trait that would be honed and strengthened over the course of my life: survival. I regarded my skillset as virtuous. I became compliant, resilient, and downright charismatic. I adapted to my new surroundings, making friends and easily fitting into my new, popular scene. I remember once describing myself to a therapist as a chameleon, and thinking that this was an admirable accessory to my social bag of tricks. The ability to transform in order to blend in however, entailed selling my soul on some level. Often, this included the use of alcohol and drugs. As I struggled to belong and simultaneously anesthetize my fear and sadness, I surrendered little pieces of myself along the way. I needed to be in control of an uncontrollable situation, and being a chameleon was my armor. My resolve to be a part of all experiences, to be "center stage", was crucial to my continuing vitality. I was vivacious, engaging, hilariously funny, and friendly; in short, "the life of the party." These attributes have carried me through my adolescence and the better part of my adulthood with a fair amount of success, albeit not without a great deal of suffering, depression, and emptiness. They were coping mechanisms, masks I wore to diminish and hide my feelings of vulnerability and uncertainty, from myself and everyone around me. Of course, I did not recognize or accept my behavior as refusal to face my pain. I didn't even recognize my pain, so I certainly wasn't ready to acknowledge my behavior.

As the first born of my parents' offspring, I had unconsciously appropriated their role as parents when they divorced. That is to say, I appointed myself the unsolicited protector, caregiver, and parent not only for my sister and brother but also to a certain extent for my other younger stepsiblings who lived under the same roof. I guess, from my narrow and immature adolescent perspective, I assumed that since they had been incapable of succeeding in their marriage, they were probably ill-suited to perform their parental duties adequately as well. It isn't until now that I realize this "noble responsibility" was not mine to assume. It has made for cosmic discord with my two, blood-related siblings. The unintentional arrogance of believing my parents were "suddenly incompetent", and that I was wiser, more adept, and stronger than they, disrupted the natural balance of things. It gave me a false attitude of superiority that undermined my true place in the world and the chance for a genuinely harmonious relationship with each of them. That same posture wreaked havoc on any hopes of having a naturally loving, humble, give-and-take bond with my sister and brother. From the time I took the unknowing decision to override my parents, competition between the three of us was born, as we instinctively vied for our proper place: equality. As I exhibited control, judgment, and criticism (what I believed was taking care of them), they subconsciously rejected and resented my unwanted efforts to replace our parents. It is only now, through much work, soul-searching, and meditation that I have come to know this all came from an unconscious place, for all of us. None of us knew better. We were all trying to do the best we could in order to avoid falling off the cliff.

I began working as a waitress at Howard Johnson's as soon as I started my junior year at Toms River High School South. I had just turned sixteen. Financial independence became a driving force in my attitude toward authority as well as an infrastructure for my rebellious antics. Having my own money enabled me to call my own shots. I bought and paid off a brand new Ford Pinto during my senior year in high school, which further broadened my capacity for spontaneous jaunts. I would think nothing of driving with friends (through the night) down to the Florida Keys for a four-day weekend. The combination of money and transportation created a slippery slope, which would eventually become unmanageable.

My last two years of high school were a dysfunctional balance of top-level, competitive gymnastics combined with alcohol and drugs. My lifetime participation in sports and "athlete's mentality" could well have been what saved me from hardcore addiction and self-destruction. An inclination toward impetuous audacity accompanied my lifestyle. Household rules, including bedtimes and curfews, were a formality that begged to be disregarded by my sister and me (we were inseparable partners in crime during this period).

We lived in a large, two-story house, with six kids and two newlywed parents who went to bed around 8:30 every night. My room and my stepbrother's room were the only ones on the first floor. Mine, in particular, offered effortless escapes, with double-hung windows (conveniently) opening directly onto the front porch. Weather never deterred us, but in the summertime there were no holds barred.

Not too far from our house were the *Pine Barrens*, a vast forest of mostly indigenous "scrub pines," that stretches across a large part of South Jersey's unpopulated geography. Inside the part of the Barrens nearest to where we lived were *the Cranberry Boggs*. This place occupied hundreds of acres and included an intricate system of small dams and bodies of water, which had been effectively designed for the cultivation and harvest of cranberries. At one time it was one of the primary suppliers of cranberries to Ocean Spray. Double Trouble, as it was (ironically) named, is now a state park, but at the time it belonged to my stepfather's family. We behaved as if we had diplomatic immunity when it came to our proprietary attitude regarding the premises. If we went in the daytime, we would wash our hair in the small waterfalls the dams produced, and sunbathe and drink beer for hours on the sandy shoals that lined the pristine (Coca Cola colored) cedar water that rushed by. It was heavenly. We weren't derelicts or vandals. This was a special place for us, and we always treated it with great respect. Nonetheless, plenty of law breaking went on: dropping by for nocturnal bonfires, skinny-dipping, or ice skating, depending on the time of year.

We would exit from my bedroom window, walk down the street, and get picked up by friends. The remainder of the night had no time restraints. We often got home right before dawn. There never seemed to be any authorities to curb our untamed behavior: no police, security guards, or parents. This encouraged our natural teenage aspiration to constantly "outdo" ourselves. There were other, regular breaking-and-entering escapades on private properties, including but not limited to the swimming pools of the Toms River Country Club and "the Herrings" (not sure of the spelling). The latter venue, we believed at the time to be the residence of a U.S. senator (research for this book did not reveal any authentication for the existence of this person, but we sure did swim in his pool!). There were scads of tempting addresses; the more risky they were to access, the better. In the winter we would go over to the affluent

seaside beach towns of Mantoloking and Bay Head
for excitement. We would let ourselves into summer
residences of friends' relatives, crank up the fireplace
and entertain ourselves amongst sheet-covered furnishings, without thinking twice.

My last two years of public high school were
one continuous blur, literally and figuratively.
Scholastically, it was a breeze compared to my previous eleven years in a private school that had a
much higher, more competitive academic bar. With
no real effort required, and no parental oversight
or structure to speak of, I skipped school regularly,
accumulating bad habits and receiving positive reinforcement for negative behavior. By this I mean that
truancy, as well as indulging in regular alcohol con-
sumption and recreational drugs had little or no
effect on my academic performance. I had found
the perfect recipe for future failure. I graduated with
straight A's only to flounder my way toward a mid-
dle-of-the-road state university.

I worked my way up from "HoJo's" to bringing
in over $500 a day in tips at a high-end restaurant
in Monmouth County. Once again, having my own
money, and plenty of it, afforded me the capability
of making my own choices. My first attempt at college would turn out to be a blip on my screen. It was
a short-lived milestone, which materialized against

most odds: the absence of guidance or advice, my apathy toward authority, and the "fly by the seat of my pants" doctrine I had assumed. Somewhere, in the back of my mind, I embraced the attitude: "If I'm payin', I'm sayin'." In other words, I entered college with the smugness of a person who was quite accustomed to doing whatever the hell she wanted, without consequences, because I was footing my own bill.

It didn't take long for reality to smack some sense into me. I had a non-existent work ethic when it came to attending and studying for classes. Sustaining and reinforcing the same modus operandi I had adopted in high school, I took full advantage of the on-campus "Rathskellar" (and the legal drinking age of eighteen). I rarely went to class, partied with reckless abandon, and ultimately took an extended "spring break" vacation to the Florida Keys with my frat-president boyfriend. The trip lasted from late March until June. Upon re-entry from the stratosphere, I returned home to find a letter from the Dean of Students, informing me that my priorities were clearly out of alignment and that I was no longer permitted to matriculate at their institution.

I may have spoken earlier as to what I believe the bi-product of insecurity, anger, and shame to be. My rebellion took on the size and power of a runaway train. No one could (or would) stop me, nor would I stop myself. How does the saying go? "A rolling stone gathers no moss"? Maybe if I kept moving I wouldn't feel the pain.

In the summer of '77, I gleefully entered the disco circuit at its inception. I dedicated my existence to working all day as a waitress and partying HARD every night, all the while perfecting my "Hustle" and "Latino" dance moves. I had a sizeable roster of regular bars and nightclubs to frequent, all pertaining to the budding underbelly of the disco society, of which I had become a fairly well-known member. Life under anesthesia is always fun and perfect, with no repercussions or consequences . . . until the anesthesia wears off. This would not happen for decades.

3

Saturday Night Fever, The Extended Version

Winter 1978, Acapulco, Mexico

I t was bound to happen. At some point, during my three-month stint as a "disco diva," I met the lead singer of a popular live band, The Originals International, who played in one of the nightclubs I patronized. The members of the band were from all different parts of the world, which explained why they were also able to score some fairly impressive gigs in the Philippines, Mexico, and Japan, among other exotic venues (at least for me). After finishing up their summer at the Jersey Shore, I promptly packed some things and left with my new man to continue their tour. He was a year older than my father, at the time.

The band worked its way across the country, finishing their U.S. leg in San Francisco, before continuing on to the Philippines for an extended engagement during the holiday season of 1977. I'm not sure I even gave any thought as to whether I should have continued on to the Orient with them. In my mind, there was no reason not to go. After all, I wasn't doing anything else that week (a mindset I maintained and joked about for years). It was a small-scale "rock star" lifestyle and I loved it.

All the other members of the band were married, and I got along fantastically with the wives (from here on, I will include myself under the heading "wives" for simplicity). In retrospect, I guess they were a replacement for my family. It was a relief to be the youngest, by several years, and it felt like a big group of fun, older brothers and sisters, who happened to be almost famous and who received red-carpet treatment wherever they went.

The band performed (and stayed) at the Manila Hotel. I imagine they had been hired with the intent of stretching out the hotel's celebration of its formal re-opening in October of that same year. The hotel is an historic landmark and the oldest premiere hotel in the Philippines. It was originally constructed in 1909 to rival Malacañang Palace, the official residence of the President of the Philippines. To describe this completely renovated, five-star property as opulent would be an understatement. We were there for the month of December and through New Year's Eve. At the age of nineteen, I had never before experienced such old-world lavishness.

As entertaining and action-packed as the celebrity scene had seemed in the U.S. and the Far East, my life's destiny would be instantly and irrevocably altered the moment I hit terra firma at the band's next venue, Acapulco, Mexico. They had a two-year contract at The Plaza, a beautiful, upscale hotel at the base of *Costera Miguel Alemán*, the main drag, which was peppered one raging discotheque after another. Did I mention it was 1978? The disco world was about to explode, and Acapulco was at its epicenter.

The first year was like a dream. It was not the band's first time in Acapulco, closer to their fourth or fifth. The boys were well known and had a solid fan base. The trumpet player was Mexican, but they all spoke Spanish. Everyone was comfortable with the culture and the accommodations. At this point, I began to feel like a celebrity. We paid for nothing and signed for everything: food, cocktails, laundry, and dry cleaning. It was all included in the band's contract.

The hotel staff bent over backwards to attend to our every need, all the time, especially the wives.

The girls and I spent our days by the pool, reading books or playing backgammon with local, leather-faced elders, who gathered daily, with their stogies and their coffee, where the pool deck met the edge of the beach. There was a tournament available at all times for anyone who was interested. We all became expert players. To this day, I can beat almost anyone who challenges me to a game of backgammon, except, of course, my oldest daughter!

I do not exaggerate when I say we drank practically every day. If we weren't at The Plaza, we had other options. There were regular daytime haunts where "the beautiful people" gathered: Villa Vera, The Princess Hotel, or any number of private residences in and around Las Brisas, an exclusive, cliff-side community south of Acapulco proper. Invitations were plentiful and continuous. There were always several appearances and social events to choose from, day and night. Cocktails usually began poolside around 4 or 5 p.m., no matter where we found ourselves (keep in mind, we usually didn't wake up until about 2 p.m.). Because we were on the Pacific coast, the sun didn't set until about 9 p.m., leaving plenty of time to rub elbows with local and international people of interest. There was never a shortage of "Hollywood and New York royalty" during the disco boom in Acapulco. Regardless of where we were, an "always attentive" wait staff, whose raison d'être was to ensure that we were never without an exotic cocktail, fresh oysters on the half shell, or ceviche, was a basic part of the background scenery. Talk about the beautiful art of doing nothing; we were like Hemingway's "idle rich," but without the trust funds.

Naptime came around 9 or 9:30 p.m. and lasted at least two hours. Around 11 p.m. or midnight, we would start getting ready to make our nightly appearance at any one of many discos. Each club had a particular night or two when it was "the place to be seen." The wives were our own entity, with our own following. We rarely went to see our boys perform. We had "a public" to address. We had standing reservations (tables) at the edge of the dance floor in every major nightclub, on any given night of the week. All we had to do was call ahead. There was always plenty of champagne, for which we never paid; although, my drink of choice at the time was Scotch. We tore up the dance floor and partied until dawn most nights, as if it was our job. Basically, it was. We even had a seamstress who regularly created one-of-a-kind "costumes" for us to wear; the more outrageous, the better.

One day, about a year into my sojourn, I was walking along the beach when someone approached me and asked if I wanted to do a print ad for Coppertone suntan lotion. Insert canned response: "Why not? I'm not doing anything else this week, ha, ha, ha . . ." I spent the week doing various photo shoots and publicity engagements for the company. When the time came to get paid, I couldn't believe how much they gave me! It's important to point out that, although I wasn't a professional model or anything close, Mexico and the U.S. had not yet entered into the NAFTA agreement. I quickly discovered that anything American, or "American looking," including attractive women with blond hair and light features, could command top dollar.

My mind started to spin. I was bored to death with doing nothing. The "jet-set" life had lost its luster. At the same time, the band's bassist and his wife were having marital troubles and were in the process of getting divorced. Annette was a stunning Texas blond who also had several modeling jobs in Acapulco. After not too much brainstorming, we decided to leave everything and go to Mexico City in pursuit of a potentially lucrative modeling opportunity. There was no trepidation involved. We basically made the decision and left the next day.

4

Bright Lights, Hot Nights

Late Spring, 1979, Mexico City, Mexico

Although we had made our decision based on becoming successful models, another opportunity presented itself simultaneously. At the same exact time, the Originals International trumpet player's wife approached Annette and me with a proposition. Jeannie Nelson was a fairly well known personality in Mexico's entertainment world. She was a statuesque blond from Wisconsin, who, for the last decade or so, had been capitalizing on the enormous marketing trend for American product endorsement.

Jeannie had made a killing in the modeling sector, but in recent years had experienced tremendous success with her own spectacular, a Las Vegas-type show based in Mexico City. She would appear in posh nightclubs, performing two shows a night. Once a year she took the show on the road, making appearances all over the country. The performance was extravagant. It was a big money maker with big financial backers. No expense was spared in its production. It had a full band, several backup singers and dancers, and elaborate costumes, which were changed many times during the show. Jeannie had been looking for two new additions to the roster for quite some time. Acquiring American talent that looked like her would boost the show's marketability even more. Neither Annette nor I had any experience whatsoever in show business, but we did have two things: years of childhood dance lessons and the bravura required to try anything new. It would be an auxiliary source of income and adventure. We accepted her offer.

Everything fell into place from that moment on. We found an agent and the modeling jobs started rolling in. We were paid almost whatever we asked. It was unbelievable. At the same time there were intensive rehearsal sessions as we learned the show's choreography as well as the mechanics involved in split-second, backstage costume changes. It was an instant whirlwind of change. We were only affected in the sense that it was a prolonged adrenaline rush. Everything was new for us: the culture, the language, our jobs, and above all, our lifestyle. We were in charge and in high demand, a heady position to be in, at any age.

Within no time we had a three-floor penthouse near the Zona Rosa, one of the best real estate locations in the city. To this day I have never lived in such opulence. The elevator opened on the top floor of the building, inside our apartment. It was professionally decorated and furnished, with sumptuous and impeccable taste. No detail had been overlooked. All the floors and bathrooms were marble. The kitchen was state of the art, although our full-time maid was the one who spent most of the time in it, as she did almost all of the cooking. There were two master suites on the second floor that followed the plush standard set on the first floor. The third floor, had one sole bedroom, completely mirrored (walls and ceiling), with a round, king-sized bed in the middle. I don't think either one of us ever used that room, but it certainly became a conversation piece! With more work (and money) than we knew what to do with, we entertained and luxuriated in this dream pad for two years. Annette was twenty-three and I hadn't even turned twenty-one!

There were print ads, TV ads, billboards, and runway modeling gigs, along with nocturnal engagements and the sporadic excitement of being on tour. We would work for a few months and then travel, in style, spending all the money we had earned, every time. There was no concern or planning for the future. It was life entirely in the present moment. We met a lot of high-profile people and made a lot of friends, some of whom I count in my circle of dear, lifetime relationships to this day.

About a year into our modeling and show business careers, we found ourselves rehearsing choreography in preparation for the months-long tour we were about to begin. Jeannie had rented a huge, fully mirrored space that was part of a sprawling health club in the heart of Colonia Roma Sur. We spent about a week at that gym, working on the somewhat complex dance moves and costume changes involved in the new show. During that time we met the owners of the health club, two brothers, Javier and Alejandro, each extraordinarily handsome and charismatic in his own right. My girlfriend started dating the older brother, Javier, and shortly thereafter, I began a relationship with Alejandro. I had no idea that in the not-too-distant future he would become my husband and the father of my two beautiful daughters.

Each (spontaneous) step that manifested for me flowed in seemingly effortless succession. In hindsight, although I didn't take stock at the time, I now realize that from the moment I arrived in Mexico, I received continuous reinforcement and affirmation from "the powers that be"—as if all the tollbooths had opened up for me to sail through without paying; as if the Universe had conspired to propel my success. There was never any doubt. I was exactly where I belonged. I felt totally at home, as if, in another (or many) past lives, I had been a part of the indigenous fabric that formed the creation of this culture.

By the end of my second year in Mexico City, Alejandro asked me to marry him. I had a few hurdles to jump over, as his mother had made it clear to me that she didn't like or trust me (or any other American women). She was a strong-willed matriarch who was used to having her way. All four of her children marched to her drum. It would take some doing to win her over, but I was head over heels in love with her son, so I had to figure it out. Step one: I retired from modeling. At least that took me out of the "prostitute" category, in her eyes. Step two: I began "pre-cana" classes with a priest who worked in the church where we wanted to marry, Nuestra

Señora de Fatima. I didn't have a Catholic bone in my body, but it was important to Alejandro (not to mention his mother), so I acquiesced. I wouldn't learn that I didn't have to "sacrifice who I was" in order to be accepted, recognized, and loved until some thirty-five years later. It's a powerful lesson and one with which, I suspect many people struggle, at some point in their lives.

It took about a year, but in the spring of 1981, I married my Mexican Adonis in a bona fide wedding extravaganza, set on the full city-block grounds on which the family's health club and respective homes were found. Most of my family from the States came to the wedding. It was a lovely, memorable event. I felt like I was truly living in a fairy tale . . . for the time being.

5

Mount Olympus

August, 1981, Mexico City, Mexico

I had been on a three-year roll of good fortune and
visionless bliss ever since I arrived in Mexico. In
a sense it seemed like four separate lifetimes: being
ousted from college, touring with a rock band, modeling and show business, and then marriage. These
all seem like extreme, unrelated and radical events,
but each one had somehow seamlessly flowed into
the other. From my perspective only good things had
happened for me, despite the fact there had been no
conscious planning or decision-making on my part.
There had been no awareness and no pause for gratitude. I took things for granted and clearly did not

pay one iota of attention to my actions or my choices. I didn't cherish my life, what I had, what I did, or with whom I was doing it. Being disconnected from one's feelings pretty much guarantees one's inability to manage unexpected adversity, the kind from which none of us are spared, at some point in our lives. Given this precarious blueprint, any sort of unforeseen crisis could come along and bring me to my knees. Still, I would remain blissfully unaware and unscathed for several more years.

And so, after a leisurely, extended honeymoon in Europe, Alejandro and I returned to begin our "real lives." Most of our friends owned publicity agencies, were involved in filmmaking, or were in the forefront of the computerized television production industry. It was the '80s and we were in Mexico. There was a lot of money and even more drugs . . . more specifically, cocaine. We were insulated from our own lifestyle by a network of housekeepers, gardeners, etc. We didn't need to accept a lot of responsibility because there were others who could assume that role for us. The family business health club was in cruise control. It required a fair amount of attention, but not hard work.

Up until my children were born there was literally no reason for me to exhibit any type of moderation (or self-preservation, for that matter). As I contemplate the impulsive foolhardiness by which I lived, I am positive it was a good thing my children came along. Their existence generated a new wave of responsibility and self-restraint in my world.

Stefani Victoria appeared in April of the following year, and like most babies, exponentially changed the lives of both her parents for the better. It was an instant shift in priorities and lifestyles. It felt good, and Lord knows I needed the rest! Elizabeth Susanna was born less than two years after her sister. We were an official family. I had plenty of time to dedicate to my daughters and little else with which to concern myself. I now realize how lucky I was to have been able to give them so much of my attention when they were babies. Literally every other aspect of my life was done for me: the day-to-day running of the house, grocery shopping, cooking, and cleaning.

All of my girlfriends had a comparable scenario. We all had two to three babies that were of similar ages. There were formal luncheons at any one of our homes at least two times a week. Everyone had cooks and service staff, and most everyone had a driver. We all brought our children and respective nannies. It was a perfect set-up: a built-in, supervised playgroup and a social event that lasted for hours. It was part of our weekly routine. Weekends were more of the same, except the husbands were included and we generally left the city for someone's vacation home or hacienda.

None of these rituals prevented us from accepting invitations to movie or theater premiers, grand openings of nightclubs, or gala events, which also occurred regularly at any time during the week.

One of our favorite, regular weekend retreats was Hacienda San Gabriel de las Palmas. Situated on one hundred and twenty-six acres in the central mountains of Mexico, its construction was commissioned by Hernán Cortés in 1529 to be used as his headquarters during his conquest of Mexico. Luckily for us, Jorge Fenton, a dear friend and well-known jeweler from Mexico City, privately owned the hacienda at the time. He was one of the first people I met when I started modeling, and ironically was also the father of one of my most cherished friends to this day, Juan Fenton. I used to laughingly refer to Don Jorge as *the Mexican Hugh Hefner* and this property as the *South of the Border Playboy Mansion*. This wasn't at all far from reality. "HSG" had a full-time staff in charge of keeping the grounds and bedroom suites in an impeccable state of readiness for any occasion at any time. Over the course of the '80s decade, we staged plenty of parties, galas, and events there, as did Don Jorge. But by far, my fondest recollections are the most mundane. These are memories of us living our lives and not giving much thought to the future. We simply enjoyed each other's company in the midst of what happened to be palatial surroundings. Oftentimes we would pack up our cars on a Friday afternoon and make the two-hour trip out of the city, winding our way along the sinuous, rustic highway, which traversed the vivid purple and green volcanic mountains that stood between paradise and us. It was best when it was just the family: Jorge, Juan, Francisca (my adored friend of whom I will speak more), Alejandro, and me with our combined brood, who were like sisters, and inseparable. We ate every meal together at an enormous rectangular table, which at the time was set up in the main building on a spacious, al fresco terrace. There was absolutely nothing pretentious about these end-of-the-week gatherings. They were comprised of keeping company with treasured friends and watching our five girls grow up. It was the healthiest, happiest part of our existence at the time.

The expansive, perfectly manicured estate was at our disposal and as much a playground for us, as it was for our daughters. Most of our time was spent around the sprawling swimming pool, which boasted two islands at its center, one connected by irregular granite steppingstones and the other by a small, arched stone bridge. The bigger island had an enormous, verdant tabachín. This regal tree bloomed with vibrant orange flowers and provided soothing shade under which the girls enjoyed many a nap as babies. The sunken canteen could be accessed from the outside of the pool as well as from inside the pool itself. A line of eight immersed barstools framed the edge of the bar. Swimmers could get to each of the islands independently and wind up at the bar for a cocktail or snack without ever leaving the pool. It was a self-contained, aquatic esplanade, lending itself to myriad activities: games, adventure, music, dancing, and theatrical performances by the girls. With a full-service restaurant located in the main building, that was pretty much operational day and night, we wanted for nothing. It's not difficult to imagine how we spent entire days there, often until it was time for the children to go to bed.

HSG has since been converted into a five-star boutique hotel, owned and run by Juan. It is the well-kept secret of many an international jetsetter, as well as a favorite haunt for exotic U.S. yoga retreats and health and wellness conferences. It has also served as the location for the filming of several A-list movies and music videos.

Note: *The hacienda (HSG) has a special place in my heart. It is my wish, when I depart from this world, that my ashes be scattered, along with those of Don Jorge and other family members, at the base of the majestic, centenarian ceiba tree, located near the back entrance of the property.*

My principles and priorities had certainly changed for the better with the birth of my children, but the dynamic of our social circle remained focused on the high life. With the exception of daytime hours when the children were present, alcohol, marijuana, and cocaine were always available. I am amazed I survived the decade. As a matter of fact, many friends and acquaintances did not. Some overdosed or committed suicide in other ways, some had heart attacks. Cocaine is a nasty, dangerous substance, and it had a solid place in our lifestyle. As I write this, I am instantly exhausted and grateful. This much I know to be true about my life: "There but for the Grace of God go I" (attributed to John Bradford). Although I could have considered myself an atheist at the time, on some level I must have acknowledged the existence of an omnipotent force. I have always been protected and guided by something much greater and more powerful than myself, even if it was in spite of myself.

I have come to believe strongly in reincarnation. I am confident that we are brought into this life to overcome obstacles and in turn learn lessons that, for whatever reason, we were unable to grasp the last time they presented themselves. I have no doubt that this is an unending process of personal evolution and growth, resulting from our experiences, none of which are ever coincidental. Often, we are unable or unprepared to recognize a learning opportunity when it shows up. Sometimes it is too painful or frightening. This explains why certain scenarios and situations occur time and time again during our lives. Their purpose is to lead us toward self-realization. They may even be carried on to subsequent lifetimes until we "get it." One thing is for sure: we get plenty of "taps on the shoulder" along the way. If we choose to ignore the signs, or are too inattentive to realize there is a choice to be made, a teachable moment will eventually be hurled at us with all the force of the Almighty.

6

"An Act Of God"

September, 1985. Mexico City, Mexico

By the time my daughters, Stefani and Elizabeth, were three and almost two, our family had hit our stride. We had a routine and life was fairly predictable and uneventful. Alejandro would wake up in the morning and walk across the property to work at the club, on the other side of the block. I would feed the girls breakfast and wait for my nanny/housekeeper, Irene, to arrive so that I too, could cross the property and spend my morning taking advantage of the luxury facilities of the club: weights, aerobics classes, swimming pool, steam bath, coffee shop.

My sister-in-law, Lupita, owned a small, private
nursery school located within the same compound as
the health club and our homes. Irene would dress the
girls in their starched and pressed uniforms and walk
them around the block to attend morning classes at
Kinder Condesa.

At 2 p.m. every day, we would all independently
converge at home for lunch, where Irenita would
serve us the delicious meal I had requested earlier that
morning. I would spend the afternoon playing and
relaxing with the girls and Alejandro would occasion-
ally go back to work. To say that life was convenient
and peaceful would have been an inaccurate description. It was blissful. I had been living in Mexico for
seven years now. I was so comfortable and "at home"
in this country and in this culture that it was almost as
if I had never lived anywhere else. If it weren't for the
summer forays to the Jersey Shore (partially because
I never surrendered my "tourist status," and had to
leave the country every one hundred and eighty days),
I could have forgotten about my family and friends in
the U.S. completely. That's how disconnected I was.

It was around 8 a.m. on the 19th of September. It's
easy to remember the date because the day before had
been my birthday. As usual, I was making breakfast
for my little chickadees. They had asked for pancakes,
a special treat for my birthday. The day was clear and

sunny, and about 72 degrees with no humidity. It was like most any other day, so beautiful that it was difficult to ever wake up in a bad mood. I stood in my second-story, sun-drenched kitchen overlooking the sprawling, lush gardens the family shared. Stefani and Elizabeth sat at the counter chatting and gurgling happily as I prepared their favorite breakfast. Even their father ("Apu") was going to come home from the club to join us.

Suddenly there was a strong rumble throughout the entire house. It was more of a "feeling" than a sound, which transformed into a deafening noise of creaking, twisting metal, crumbling concrete, and imploding edifices. I knew instantly that this was an earthquake . . . a big one. I snatched the girls from the kitchen counter, practically by their shirts, and clutched one in each arm as I stood in the frame of my kitchen door. The seismic activity seemed endless, though later reports confirmed that it had lasted less than four minutes. Continuous, terrified screams and sirens pierced the air. At some point I noticed the air we were breathing was thick with the smell of gas, adding a whole new level of terror. Outside the walls of the family estate, chaos and destruction had occurred. Luckily, all our homes and the club within the compound were unscathed. Most others in our neighborhood had not been so lucky. Colonia Roma was one of the hardest hit areas of this natural disaster. Many apartment buildings, offices, and businesses were leveled. The cross street at the end of our block had collapsed into the earth and was about eight feet below the level of our street. In the club, the indoor pool had lost half its contents. The water had actually sloshed out of the pool like a huge wave! People ran and shrieked hysterically in the streets. Still squeezing the girls in a death-grip hold, I walked downstairs from my house to the middle of the garden, where I sat in shock, silently waiting for Alejandro to appear. I tried to make sense of what had happened while at the same time my mind raced, thinking of how we could flee the city during such mayhem. It would take days for us to leave and seek refuge in Cuernavaca, the beautiful City of Eternal Spring, about an hour south of Mexico City in the mountains. Because it was a healthier, unpolluted environment, as well as considerably safer in terms of crime, Cuernavaca would become our permanent residence.

Such was the wreckage, the instant homelessness and despair of so many thousands of people in our midst, that we decided to offer the club as a refuge for entire families who had been thrust onto the streets from one moment to the next. Alejandro and Javier had fortunately just completed the construction of an enormous second gymnasium on the premises. It could easily accommodate over two hundred people. And so we opened our doors, to the elderly, newborn babies, and everyone who fit. There was running water and bathrooms in the club, which was a godsend. We received donations from countless, unknown sources; blankets, canned goods, disposable diapers, and anything else that helped to sustain the masses. It was amazing to witness the dauntless, inextinguishable determination of the human spirit in action. I was proud to be a part of it. It also helped to distract us all from the epic catastrophe we were experiencing.

After four or five days, people were able to leave the Club for provisional housing that had been set up around the city. It was our opportunity to make our exit. My grandparents had purchased a vacation home in Cuernavaca about a year and a half earlier. My grandmother, Namu (Elizabeth Chadbourne DuBois, to whom this book is dedicated), and I enjoyed a close lifetime friendship. She and Jim married when I was two. He never had children of his own, but took his role as grandfather seriously. It was Jim who taught me how to drive and sail a boat, among many other important milestones in my life. Because of the geographic circumstances pertaining to both my biological grandfathers, he was the person I always considered to be my true grandfather.

Namu and Jim both loved to paint as a hobby, and at the time Cuernavaca had quite an established artist community. There were art schools and classes readily available, and plenty of Americans to make their transition comfortable. The town also boasted many historical monuments, churches, and sprawling haciendas, all with rich historical backgrounds of great interest to them. This, along with the consistently spectacular year-round weather, the magnificent foliage, and the opportunity to spend extended winter vacations with us, had made the real estate purchase an easy decision.

My grandparents had intentionally chosen a large house with a swimming pool and four large bedrooms in order to encourage long-term visits. On the tail of the incredible force of nature we had survived, this home spontaneously became a perfect and mutual blessing for us all! We moved right in. I was able to take care of my grandparents (not that they needed it at the time) and they had the joy of experiencing their great granddaughters on a daily basis. Once more, the stars had aligned. Once again we fell in stride. Alejandro had an easy, daily commute back and forth to the club, and we enrolled the girls in a wonderful Montessori School not too far from our new home.

There is no doubt that this was far more than a lovely coincidence. It was a miracle. Yet, looking back, as difficult as it is to admit, I had taken it all for granted.

We plugged along, in cruise control for about a year and a half. Namu and I loved each other's company and often ran errands together. One day we were in *el centro* to pick up some reading glasses she had ordered, and to swing by *el mercado* to purchase our weekly supply of fresh fruits and vegetables. As we walked from one vendor to the next, along uneven slabs of cement sidewalk, Namu lost her footing and fell down. We had always marveled at how spry and agile she was for her age, but this time she couldn't get up. I ended up having to call the Red Cross to come and pick her up.

In Mexico, particularly in more remote towns and small cities, the Red Cross acts much in the same way as EMTs in the U.S. That is to say, they are the first responders whenever there is an accident or catastrophe. They also have a headquarters, to which victims requiring emergency care are taken, almost without exception, before they are brought to any hospital. The highly trained personnel of the Red Cross dress in camouflage uniforms and military boots, which could likely be a bit unnerving, if not downright scary to the unknowing eye of a foreign tourist. We rode together in the back of the

ambulance as I tried unsuccessfully to calm down
my sweet grandmother. She was beside herself with
a combination of pain and terror. It was difficult to
keep her from hyperventilating. Against the strong
medical advice of Red Cross volunteers, we asked to
be taken home and not to their headquarters or the
hospital. At this point, we didn't know exactly what
Namu's degree of injury was. The plan was to get her
in bed and get her calm and comfortable. This way
she could address this in her own way: by praying.

It should be mentioned that both my grandparents were devout Christian Scientists. Christian
Science is a set of beliefs and practices developed
in nineteenth century New England by Mary Baker
Eddy. In essence, practitioners believe that reality
is purely spiritual and therefore it is our thoughts
that govern our experiences; mind over matter, so to
speak. Using the skillset of prayer, it is the Christian
Scientists' conviction that any illness or malady can
and will be cured by prayer alone. It is not necessarily
that they are vehemently opposed to modern medicine and doctors, rather they simply do not recognize
them as viable options for any medical issue.

Less than an hour later, I once again summoned
the Red Cross. Namu lost consciousness because of the
intense pain she experienced. When they arrived they
needed to act quickly to neutralize her discomfort. She

was in her late seventies and had never seen the inside of a doctor's office or taken so much as an aspirin. The multiple injections of morphine she needed in order to manage the pain undoubtedly altered her razor-sharp clarity and consciousness a great deal. This must have seemed like a nightmarish torture chamber to her. It was the first and only medicine that had ever entered her body in her entire life. She was taken directly to Red Cross headquarters, where she was examined and X-rays were taken. In short order we found out that she had not only broken her right hip but that her femur had shattered completely in half, right in the center of her quadriceps. Emergency surgery was imperative, and time was of the essence.

Because of my grandmother's fervent religious beliefs, she was beyond traumatized with the Red Cross/ambulance experience she had undergone. I then had to convince her to have emergency orthopedic surgery or she would have died. It was an agonizing episode for both of us. She felt like I was betraying her. I will never forget the look of sadness and disbelief she gave me as we wheeled her into *el Hospital Henri Dunant*. To this day it's one of the most difficult moments I've ever endured. Once she stabilized and had spoken to a surgeon, we pressured her to consent to receiving medical treatment. It took more than six hours of surgery to repair her hip and thigh.

After days in the hospital, she was finally released. My vibrant, active grandmother was now confined to a wheelchair. She wasn't used to depending on anyone and she certainly wasn't accustomed to the meds and frequent doctor appointments that came to pass. Her spirit slowly extinguished.

Not surprisingly, after three months Namu had not improved. She should've been up and walking on her own much before that, but her morale was working against her. She was depressed and felt like she had forsaken her beloved religious beliefs. This had taken a serious toll on all of us, but I imagine it particularly affected Namu and Jim's relationship and quality of life. The ordeal had surely weighed on Jim, as he had been left with no other choice but to take a quiet back seat to the drama that had unfolded. As an equally devoted Christian Scientist, I can imagine how absolutely helpless and frustrated Jim must have felt during this entire experience.

We all agreed there was no option but for them to go home to New Jersey, with Namu in a wheelchair. We didn't talk about it then, but I wonder if they knew they would remain in New Jersey for the rest of their lives, never to return to Mexico, or to their beautiful Cuernavaca home again. Jim peacefully passed away on his own birthday, less than three years after their homecoming.

7

Modern-Day Pioneers

November 1987, The Eastern Seaboard, U.S.A

This marked the beginning of the end, of sorts, as far as us living in Cuernavaca. I began to feel more and more anxious about not being able to work and bring money into the family, and Alejandro wasn't making enough for us to make ends meet. I could get a job in the States, and Alejandro could look for a better paying source of income. After much deliberation and soul-searching, we (begrudgingly) decided to give the U.S. a try, and in late November of '87, we moved to New Jersey, on a quest for a better life.

My husband found work fairly quickly through a connection of my sister's. Her then-boyfriend's father owned Viking Construction, a company that was locally known and respected for creating high-end, impeccably built homes. At the time, there was an incredible boom for building, and the company had more contracts than it could turn out. Ale hit the ground running. He had substantial experience in construction and architecture, and Mr. Tremouth taught him everything he knew. Alejandro's creativity and high standards quickly made him an indispensable asset to the company. Every day I watched my husband wake up excited to go to work. He absolutely loved what he was doing, and Mr. Tremouth consulted with him often for his ideas and approval of many projects.

But the winter season could not be avoided. The weather grew colder and more inclement each day. It would turn out to be a particularly brutal winter, with bitter cold and frequent heavy wind and snow that lasted for months. These conditions are not easy for seasoned Northeasterners to tolerate, much less those of us used to year-round spring. By mid-December, Alejandro had contracted a serious case of pneumonia. The EMO (emergency medical offices) doctor told him it was crucial that he check himself into the hospital. Unfortunately, we had no health insurance at the time, and were left with no other option but for him to stay at home.

Luckily, it was the Christmas season and I landed a full-time job at the Estée Lauder cosmetics counter at the local Mall. It couldn't have come at a more perfect time. After the usual waiting period, I received full health benefits for the whole family. I was also able to support my family for many months while Ale convalesced at home. With two little girls, it was not easy, but we made it work. While they were home, Ale took care of them as best as he could. Stefani went to first grade for a full day and we enrolled Elizabeth in nearby Beachwood Nursery School. With the exception of the discomfort of Alejandro's real illness, the wind was once again at our backs. Things fell into place and we sailed smoothly for quite some time.

Ale had totally recovered by early spring. By summertime he started his own construction company, "American Dream Builders." We had a good run from about June until December. He had a great team of finish carpenters, and I ran the office. We were making a better than decent living.

And then, along came another wakeup call from the Universe. The bottom fell out of the construction boom as the country slid into a recession. The jobs stopped coming in from one day to the next. To add insult to injury, I got a crippling case of pneumonia around Christmas that stopped me in my tracks. Worse news came on New Year's Eve, when Ale told me he wanted to go back to Mexico because he was terrified he might catch pneumonia from me. It was something he said he wouldn't survive a second time around. I felt like the wind had been knocked out of me. *Was he actually going to bow out when the girls and I needed him most?* In fact, he was.

There are certain times in our lives when we face crises. I didn't have the awareness at the time, that I was fully capable of doing whatever was necessary. I didn't have the emotional strength or self-confidence and I was unable to take a compassionate attitude with my husband and his logical fear of becoming ill again. My ego told me HE OWED ME. In my mind, his job was to care for the family, no matter what, and he was abandoning us. My disappointment and sadness gave way to anger. This was an emotion I could identify with. It gave me the justification I needed to make him the villain, and me the victim. With a convenient place on which to attach the blame, the foundation of our marriage began to unravel.

I shifted into survival mode. As had happened when Ale had pneumonia, I couldn't be hospitalized. But this time it wasn't because we didn't have health insurance, it was because the girls needed to be cared for. I was so weak I had to arrange for the school bus to pick them up at the end of our driveway. During the winter/spring of '89, I spent two months recuperating on the living-room couch.

Ale returned in the late spring, after I had recovered. I was resentful and bitter. In my opinion, he had not held up his end of the bargain. I would describe our marriage at this time as lukewarm at best. In hindsight, we must've had bigger fish to fry because I swept our matrimonial issues under the rug and directed my attention to our failing company. The construction business was still slow on the East Coast. We limped along, but there wasn't enough business for us to make a living.

For some time, my father had been telling us that construction work was plentiful where he lived in Jacksonville, Florida. Why didn't we move down there? This way, we could continue earning an adequate living and be close to him. It was tempting. For many years I had wanted to establish a relationship I had never had with my dad. It would be great for him to get to know his only two (at the time) granddaughters. After another session of soul searching, we decided to rent our house and move south.

Florida's standard of living was, and is to this day, considerably lower than that of the Northeast, so the little savings we had would last for a while. We rented a beautiful, sprawling ranch, about half a mile from my dad's house. It was nicer than any home I'd ever lived in: a large entry foyer with marble floor; hardwood flooring and plush, white wall-to-wall carpeting throughout; a sunken living room with wet bar; a great room with vaulted ceilings; four enormous bedrooms, two walk-in closets, and a massive marble bathroom in the master bedroom. I was excited to be able to spend time with my father and to embark on a new family adventure. Maybe it would even inject new blood into our marriage!

And so the process of my dad introducing Ale to "the right people," and setting up *American Dream Builders – South* began. If what we had been told by my father was true, Ale would soon be busier than ever and I might not even have to work. We enrolled the girls in a nearby public grammar school and optimistically poised ourselves for the next bountiful chapter of our lives.

It took about a month to sense an inkling of prejudice in the southern culture of Jacksonville. Ale couldn't seem to get work on his merit with his own company. Perhaps, we supposed, it was because people tend to go with what they know, hire the guy who built the neighbor's deck, and so forth. It's like that with construction. I must say, it took a great deal of humility and courage for Alejandro to eventually take a finish carpentry job with a well-established construction company. By the end of October, reality had crystallized. The degree of racial intolerance where we lived was appalling. We also noticed that, for some reason, there was particularly strong disdain for Mexicans. Ale was treated like an ignorant, unskilled migrant worker, and was being paid accordingly. The scope of this bigotry seemed to be prevalent. It was socially accepted and culturally embraced. We couldn't stay afloat with his meager income, so I had to look for a job. I shortly found good-paying employment as a translator at a large import/export company. The only problem was the daily two-hour commute to and from my job. Déjà vu ensued. Again, I became the sole breadwinner of the family and Ale stayed at home with the girls. Our marriage and day-to-day life became quite strained. By mid-December, six short months after uprooting the family for a pie-in-the-sky illusion, we found ourselves considering another major move. We simply couldn't earn a living where we were, and worse, there was nothing for us in New Jersey either. By process of elimination, we decided to give Mexico another go. We would return to Namu's house in Cuernavaca and Ale would resume driving back and forth to Mexico City each day to manage the club. As I reflect, I am moved by our indomitable zest for "starting over." All of us were excited to go back to Mexico. Turn the page! Next chapter! On to the next adventure!

We had a gigantic garage sale and sold a lot of our furniture. What we couldn't fit in our car, we put in storage. During the girls' Christmas vacation we drove from Jacksonville to Mexico City.

We settled back into Namu's Cuernavaca residence and enrolled the girls in a forward-thinking Montessori School. They seemed to be unaffected by the recent, frequent moves, and absolutely loved their new school. Our social connections rekindled instantly. We had many close friends in Cuernavaca who, like us, were refugees of the '85 earthquake, plus we frequently received weekend houseguests from Mexico City.

The change had been relatively seamless. Our lives were back in a groove and our calendar was full enough to keep us continuously distracted. There was one looming problem: our marriage had sustained some major, fundamental injuries. At the time, I don't think we had the tools to address these issues. We didn't seek professional help and we didn't discuss our concerns with friends. This would ultimately make it even more difficult to sever our relationship. To the outside world we appeared to be the perfect couple: attractive, fun, and stable. I, on the other hand, had begun to allow myself to face my feelings. I began to feel empty and without direction or purpose. I couldn't get a clear picture in my head of what I should be doing, but I knew there was something better, more meaningful for me in my life.

8

The Jersey Shore

Summer vacation arrived. It was time for us to go to the States for an extended stay at the Jersey Shore, as we did most summers. It was a carefree, fun time for us all. It gave me the opportunity to catch up with old friends and, most of all, family members. My girls had friends and lots of cousins they enjoyed visiting as well. My mom and stepfather were still in the home where we had grown up. It was a large, 100-year-old, six-bedroom house on the edge of the Toms River.

One hundred yards away from the house was the Beachwood Yacht Club (BYC) of which we all had been members over the years. Upon arrival, we signed Stef and Elizabeth up for the same sailing program that we had all participated in as children.

It couldn't have been more convenient. The girls would wake up in the morning, eat breakfast, and then help me make a brown bag lunch for them to take to sailing camp. Then we'd all walk down the boardwalk that framed the river, beginning in front of my mother and step-father's house and winding around a few hundred yards to the yacht club. There were about fifteen kids, all with Optimist prams in the program.

The Optimist pram is a small, single-handed sailing dinghy specifically for children up to the age of fifteen. They are usually made of fiberglass. Optimists are one of the most popular sailing dinghies in the world, used in over one hundred and twenty countries, and are one of only two yachts recognized as "International Class," exclusively for sailors under sixteen, by the International Sailing Federation. Many Olympic sailors have started their careers with Optimists.

This is relevant information because the sailing community is huge in the Toms River area. There are many yacht clubs dotting the shores of Toms River, Barnegat Bay, Seaside Park, Metedeconk River, Mantoloking, and Bay Head. Barnegat Bay is a small

brackish arm of the Atlantic Ocean, approximately
forty-two miles long. It stretches along the coast of
Ocean County, New Jersey, and is separated from
the Atlantic by a long barrier island, home to the
resort towns of Seaside Heights and Seaside Park.
All fourteen of the local sailing yacht clubs located
around the waters of the Barnegat Bay belong to the
Barnegat Bay Yacht Racing Association (BBYRA),
which was established in 1914.

Barnegat Bay has produced countless Olympic-
level and "America's Cup" sailors over the past several decades. Each yacht club has a sailing program,
with inter-club races for kids as well as regular,
BBYRA weekend regattas for the more seasoned,
die-hard sailors like my parents, brothers, and sisters. We were all involved on some level and enjoyed
either watching or participating in the Saturday races,
which were always followed by an evening dinner
at the hosting yacht club, that changed each week.
There were live bands, dancing, and socializing. It
was a healthy and extremely fun setting.

The BYC sailing program would hold "mini-re-
gattas" every day, right in front of my mom and
step-father's house. It was fun to sit on their deck
and watch the kids race. By the end of the summer
they would have full command of the sailing tech-
niques necessary to sail any simple boat. Once a

week there were interclub races with other yacht clubs. The program lasted most of the summer, and the girls loved it.

My daughters had made many friends during the summer, and when the end of August rolled around, they began their "campaign" to convince me to stay and allow them to enroll in the local public grammar school. I was prompted to think. My marriage to Ale had steadily decomposed since my bout with pneumonia. There was no animosity between us, but there was little of anything else either. We didn't fight, but my respect and trust in my husband had left the day he left me to deal with my illness and our two small girls. He had long since stopped being an equal partner in my mind. I felt like I couldn't depend on him. As far as I could see, there was little difference in staying with him or being without him. This was a chance for me to go back to college and make something of myself so that I could give the girls a good life. Stef and Elizabeth had obviously become quite flexible and adept with change from all the moves we had experienced during their lives. This made my decision to ask Alejandro for a divorce and stay in New Jersey that much easier. The girls, it appeared, would be fine.

I would be remiss if I didn't take this moment to mention that, without the amazing love and support of my mother and stepfather, this huge change would not have been possible for any of us. They gave me the chance to investigate what it was that was missing in my life. They gave me the opportunity to go back to college, full-time, for the next four years, and in so doing, alter the course of the rest of my life, in a powerful way. Thank you, Nancy and Dan Crabbe, for trusting me, and my potential!

We settled into my mom and step-father's house and never went back to Mexico, at least not for a few years. I would briefly return later that year to get a few important belongings, and the girls would eventually begin spending all of their school holidays and entire summers with their father. In the meantime, I signed both of them up at Pine Beach Elementary School, Elizabeth in first grade and Stefani in third grade. It was a small, public school in a sleepy shore town, where not much happened. That was a good thing. There was no crime to speak of and most of the families were blue-collar, hardworking, and honest, with nice kids. I felt comfortable about the girls being in school there. PBES was less than half a mile from the house, so I drove the girls to school every day.

They joined the Brownies and Girl Scouts and had a lot of nice friends. I even became a Girl Scout troop leader and took them on several "out of the ordinary" trips (like spending the night in the *Tree House* at the Philadelphia Zoo). When I was sure we had all adjusted comfortably, I signed up for classes at Ocean County Community College (OCC), resuming, at thirty-two, my arduous road to a college degree, from the beginning.

9

Doctor Richards

January, 1991, Toms River, New Jersey, U.S.A.

Although my goal was to have my record
expunged at Montclair State University, and
start with a clean slate, this would take some time.
As I began the process, I discovered that it wasn't
cut and dried. MSU, not surprisingly, wanted to
conduct an intensive screening with me to confirm
that, more than thirteen years later, I had realigned
my priorities with that of a mature student, serious
about her education and degree. It was a waiting
game. I didn't want to lose momentum, so I continued on with my second semester at OCC. I wasn't
sure what I wanted to major in, but I was sure that

I wanted to maintain a connection with Mexico and its language, which I loved and missed terribly. I signed up for courses in Spanish and Science.

One morning, around the beginning of March, I got my daily phone call from Namu. I was immersed in various study groups in preparation for mid-term exams, but she had called to ask a favor. On the rare occasions that Namu solicited my help, I always did my best to oblige. In addition to our uncommonly close friendship and mutual understanding, there were other elements responsible for the strong bond we shared. As long as I could remember it seemed that her life's priority was to provide me with innumerable, rare experiences and material things, which integrally contributed to me becoming the kind of person I have become. What I have subconsciously gleaned from these countless acts of love, together with her consistent, spiritual advice and guidance, has been priceless. Even back then, I realized how fortunate I was to share this special alliance with her. I couldn't begin to repay her for what she had selflessly given me. It wouldn't be until after she was gone that I realized, in a much more literal sense, how much I would come to rely on what she had taught me. To this day, she is an incredible role model for me. She is the person who taught me how to simply, *be love*. The more engaged

I become in my spiritual endeavors, the more she continues to be an example I strive to emulate. I think and dream about her often. There is no doubt she is with me all the time!

Namu called me that day to ask me to pick her up after I finished classes for the day and take her to her final checkup with her orthopedic surgeon. More than three years earlier, Doctor Peter Richards had unquestionably saved her life. When Namu had returned to the States after a long and incomplete rehabilitation, she turned to her Christian Science roots and refused to accept being confined to a wheelchair. After three months of fierce determination and prayer, Namu had begun to walk. Things seemed okay for a short while, until one day while gardening, her leg buckled under her. She was found, barely conscious on the ground, among the plants and flowers. Evidently the hardware used to mend her fractured thighbone in Mexico had broken inside her leg, causing her femur to shatter and induce profuse internal bleeding. She needed surgery without delay. This would be the second time in her life, that my grandmother, with tremendous grace, would open her perspective beyond her Christian Science beliefs. She called upon her profound faith and was able to gather the courage and humility necessary to accept her situation and consent to medical attention, a valiant decision that prolonged her life for many, many years.

Namu obviously had no knowledge of any medical references to turn to, so my mother sought the advice of my Aunt Sarah, who had many social connections with doctors that worked at a large, nearby hospital. She recommended Doctor Peter Richards, a well-known and highly respected orthopedic surgeon. Within minutes, Namu was in an ambulance being rushed to the hospital. She was operated on, stabilized and out of bed, walking within three days. From then on, I felt a deep sense of appreciation for this physician, although I had never met him.

I had known I wanted to re-marry from the moment I asked Alejandro for a divorce. Our union had been one of real love, and our marriage of ten years had brought us happiness and two beautiful daughters. My personal opinion is that human beings in general are not wired to *mate for life*. There are, of course, those who are fortunate exceptions, however given that we are all in constant flux, experiencing continuous change (whether extreme or subtle), it is quite logical that these shifts and transformations do not necessarily occur along parallel lines. Further, when one selects a partner without first having an intimate relationship and deep understanding of themselves, it's a hopeful

gamble, at best. How can we possibly expect to successfully choose someone with whom to co-create a
harmonious, lifelong partnership if we are unaware
of *who* we are first? It happens all the time, and I'm
not so sure this is a bad thing. Each relationship
and experience that occur in our lives is designed
to give us the opportunity to learn and grow, should
we so choose. As with most things, the more chal-
lenging or difficult the test is, the more grand and
satisfying the reward. I learned many things from
Alejandro, but our time together had run its course.
This was one of many times in my life when I knew
I had to move on, not knowing why or what awaited
me. It was one of many times that I was sure to
encounter adversity and criticism from friends and
loved ones. It was one of many times when I would
face significant hardship as a result of my decisions. Yet none of these deterrents were powerful
enough to dissuade me. It was time to move on, and
I was determined to pay close attention, so as not
to choose the same kind of man. This, I believed,
would guarantee that I would avoid repeating my
previous mistakes.

Namu and I walked arm in arm into the doctor's
office, and because she had nonchalantly briefed
me in the car as to her doctor's marital status, my
interest was already piqued. Although my divorce

had not yet been finalized, my subconscious eligibility checklist was activated as I began to assess the man in front of me.

Dr. Richards was nothing like Alejandro. He was big, boisterous and very sure of himself. His extroverted, high self-esteem gave me a positive first impression, as I was deliberately browsing for traits that were unlike those of his predecessor. Moreover, the knowledge that he had saved Namu's life gave him extra clout. Peter boldly asked me out to dinner, right there in the examination room, right in front of my grandmother. Certainly, she had asked me to accompany her to her last appointment, with that exact motive. She had always been the quintessential matchmaker. She wanted everyone to have love in their lives, from the tollbooth collector on the Garden State Parkway to her orthopedic surgeon, and *most especially* her granddaughter. With her implicit approval and the stark contrast between Peter and Alejandro, I accepted.

It was a whirlwind courtship and I allowed myself to dive blindly into the fairy tale. There were gifts of cell phones, chocolates and long-stemmed roses on Valentine's Day. We took a 10-day trip to St. Thomas in March to celebrate Doctor Richard's birthday. The jewelry and perfume he presented me with, on the trip alone, were certainly extravagant.

After all, we had only been dating for two months. But what happened on our drive home from the airport when we returned was out of a movie script: We veered off the Parkway a few exits early and pulled into a car dealership, where he presented me with a brand new Range Rover! It seemed excessively generous, but I didn't resist. I kept thinking about giving my daughters a stable, worry-free life, and there was the undying gratitude for what he had done for Namu too.

I am astonished as I realize how we, as human beings, have an incredible ability to create and justify our own version of the truth. We have the capacity to selectively see, hear and experience what we want for ourselves in our lives, and to brilliantly advocate or ignore anything that could impede our pipe dreams from becoming a reality. In retrospect, I was so determined to be financially stable and have a solid structure around which I could raise my children, that I chose, not only to ignore, but effectively "hide" any downside my relationship with Peter presented. It is for this reason, I believe, that no one in my family or close circle of friends ever came to me with concerns about the dynamic of our courtship. From whatever angle I elect to look back on this chapter of my life, consciously or unconsciously, my motives for marrying Peter Richards were inauthentic – not fair to the person who, despite his own flaws, had shown up from his own personal place of genuine love.

September rolled around and the good doctor convinced me not to go back to college (red flag). Still, with one foot barely in the real world, I insisted we, including Stef and Elizabeth, live together for one full year to be sure this was the right thing for us all. Without much resistance, Peter agreed to my proposal, and in the fall of 1991 we moved to an enclave of homes that backed up to the Toms River Country Club, called Cranmoor Manor. In keeping with his, now established natural munificence, Doctor Richards redecorated and furnished the entire house to the girls' and my specifications. No expense was spared: custom furnishings, wall paper, crystal chandeliers, top of the line accoutrements of every sort. It was surreal and too good to be true. *Just keep your eyes closed, Vikki, and the bubble won't burst.*

Almost exactly a year after we had moved in, Peter asked me to marry him, accompanied by an enormous diamond ring. In my head, there hadn't been much to complain about over the past year. He had passed the litmus test. He was good company most of the time, although we didn't have much in common. He was nice to my girls, which was a must. Was I *in love* with him? No. But as long as I was going to partake in a Hollywood fantasy, I might as well subscribe to the proverb, "first time for love, second for money". We were married in November. In retrospect there had been a barrage of warning signs. It wouldn't take long for the Universe to thrust them in my face.

It has become clear to me that there are no *bad* people. We all have different levels of awareness, which fluctuate constantly. I use the analogy of a Kindergartner with my meditation students: *Do we become angry or hold a grudge against a 5-year old who doesn't know how to balance a checkbook?* He simply doesn't have the experience or the tools to have acquired that type of knowledge (awareness) yet. None of us wakes up in the morning and makes a conscious decision to be a mediocre version of ourselves. We all do the best we can, given our level of awareness at any given time. Period. After more than 27 years I can appreciate what I have learned. Simply put, the "Law of Attraction" always prevails. We receive that which we emanate. I entered this matrimony from a place of fear, from an urgency to protect myself and my children, and the belief that I was incapable of doing this alone. I deceived myself, and in turn the man I married. Sooner or later the outcome would be inevitable. In my mind, financial stability was directly linked to happiness.

It was imperative that I *live* this experience in order to learn that this belief was a fallacy.

Our honeymoon was pleasant. I successfully side-lined any intermittent thoughts that drifted into my head suggesting that I had somehow been untrue to myself, untrue to my heart, untrue to Peter. As I caught a glimpse of the lavish, financially secure lifestyle into which I had married, I (temporarily) believed that *this would be enough.* I allowed myself to be swept away. There were hot air balloon rides, shopping sprees and sumptuous dining, but the *Universe* will always triumph. The more time we spent together, the more I realized, in my heart of hearts, that I had made a mistake. Once we give ourselves permission to see the truth, we cannot "unsee it". It will stay with us and nag at us until we have the courage to surrender to our own authentic selves.

10

Refuge

Summer, 1993, Tlalpuente, Mexico City, Mexico

Although I now regard our brief union as having been an important and necessary event in my life, I began to become increasingly uncomfortable in the months that followed our honeymoon. I was no longer able to ignore thoughts and incidents that caused me to feel more and more hypocritical.

One morning, about seven months into our marriage, I decided I needed some time to clear my head and reflect on what was honestly important to me. This coincided with the annual trip my girls took to Mexico to spend the summer with their father. I packed a few things and we went to the airport. The three of us got on a plane to Mexico City. Fortunately, I had maintained a strong infrastructure of friends in Mexico over the years, among whom was Alejandro. From the time of our divorce, he and I had worked hard on remaining close, for the sake of the girls. I knew I could count on him and other dear friends to give me unconditional love and support, at any time, for any reason. Once I arrived at my best friend, Francisca's home in Mexico City, I phoned Peter and asked him to give me some time to collect my thoughts. This would turn out to be a *come to Jesus moment* that lasted for the entire summer.

Back in 1978, my love affair with Mexico was set in unexpected, irreversible motion from the moment I stepped off the plane. Almost immediately I was overcome by an undeniable feeling of having *come home*. At once I felt embraced by the people and culture, as if they had been awaiting my return. I felt safe and loved. It was a peculiar feeling at first, mainly because I had had no previous exposure to anything remotely related to this country or its language. This prompted me to contemplate the concept of *reincarnation* for the first time. How could an entire culture have instantly felt so familiar and comfortable to me? How did I willingly immerse myself in its traditions, cuisine and language in the way a person falls head over heels in love? *I must have been here in another lifetime…no, in many, many other lifetimes.* I noticed that when I met someone for the first time, we often experienced a mutual kinship. This happened time and time again. The friendships that were forged became closer and more intimate than anything I had ever known, including with my own family members and acquaintances in the United States. Given this magical, inexplicable phenomenon with which I had been blessed in my initial twelve years as a resident/ *born-again Mexican,* it is not surprising that I would turn to the friends and country of my heart for solace and support in times of trouble.

Francisca and I met in 1979 because our soon-to-be husbands were life-long friends. She was from Chile, so we were both foreigners. We were the same age, with similar interests and lived in the same neighborhood in Mexico City. Our connection was immediate. Our first two daughters were born within months of one another. Francisca had a third daughter a few years later. We spent time together practically everyday. Because the weather is predominantly spring-like and radiant all year round, we often strolled in nearby *Parque Mexico.* We also took turns making lunch for each other several times a

week. On the weekends we'd often leave the city
with Juan and Alejandro and go to *The Hacienda
San Gabriel de las Palmas,* which I have previously
described as one of my friend Juan's father's private residences. Our two families were inseparable
for more than a decade. When I divorced Alejandro
and went back to the States, it was difficult for us
all to say goodbye. For years to come, Stefani and
Elizabeth would spend all their school vacations in
Mexico, including entire summers. Fortunately, this
gave the five girls the opportunity to continue to be
part of each other's lives over the years.

The day I arrived to Mexico with my girls, it was
Francisca who received me, with open arms, into her
beautiful home in Tlalpuente. Nestled in the mountains at the southern end of Mexico City, Juan and
Francisca had built an idyllic residence, of hewn
stone, and thatched roofs with turrets. It was on a
large parcel of land with open fields in the elevated
outskirts of Mexico City. The weather was consistently crisp and sun-drenched. It was a beautiful and
comforting environment in which to seek refuge
while I gave myself the time to figure out what I was
going to do with my life. Francisca graciously invited
me to stay indefinitely, which is why I felt completely
comfortable extending my excursion for 3 months.

11

"Back To School"

Fall, 1993, Montclair State University, Upper
Montclair, New Jersey, U.S.A.

"Labor" Day had a different meaning for me
that year. I spent the better part of two days
single-handedly moving our belongings from Peter's
house back into my mom's house. I was consciously
grateful that my mom and stepfather, once again, had
received us into their home, and with no questions
asked. They were unconditionally willing to assist
us, for as long as it took, in finding our way. Peter
didn't resist the decision to divorce in any way. I
never talked to him about it, but I think that he
too, must've felt that our time together had come to

an end. Thanks to my time with Doctor Richards, I got to know myself on a deeper, more transparent level. For this I will be forever appreciative. I learned things about *me*, not all of them positive. If, for no other reason than to extract this precious nugget of wisdom that would eventually surface, my short-lived experience with Peter was well worth it.

Stef and Elizabeth began another year at Pine Beach Elementary, and I was newly free to pursue my dream of acquiring my bachelor's degree. I returned to Montclair State University that fall. It was a benchmark of determination and humility. The administration of my former Alma Mater had agreed to expunge my previous record and allow me to matriculate (from the beginning), with the goal of earning my Bachelor of Arts degree. Although I was not yet sure of what my eventual profession would be, I was positive that it would somehow involve the language and culture of Mexico. I declared a major in Spanish. This would later dovetail to include a specialization in simultaneous interpreting and translation.

The daily commute for three-plus years was harrowing, to say the least. Geographically it was an hour and a half in each direction. Depending on traffic and weather (the winters were rough), it could take up to four or five hours each way. Thankfully, I never contemplated the finish line. Had I done so, it might have been unbearable. The gratitude I felt for being afforded a second chance, together with my passion for the course content of the curriculum, made the time pass without strain. It was hard work, for sure, but the constant challenge showed me what I was capable of. The experience materialized into a radical, positive reinforcement of my self-esteem. I had been the oldest person in all of my classes, by almost fifteen years, but it was where I belonged. I never felt out of place because I finally realized there was direction in my life. By taking a full course load each semester, including summer sessions, I graduated early, summa cum laude, in mid-December of 1996.

Almost immediately after I graduated, the girls and I moved to Rumson, New Jersey, an affluent community where both my brother and sister lived with their families. I knew I would have to start working full time right away and that my siblings would prove to be a strong, loving support system for all of us. Because I had had the good fortune of attending a distinguished private school for most of my life, I knew the value of a good education. I couldn't afford private school for my daughters, but the Rumson-Fair Haven Public School district was known to be academically exceptional. When the school year began in the fall, I started my first job as a corporate interpreter/translator at a large Colombian export company in New York City. It was a great job but the long hours were taxing. I had to take an early-morning train, and sometimes I didn't get home until 8 or 9 at night. My sister was extremely generous and invaluable in helping me by taking care of the girls after school, but I wanted to find a way to participate in their lives on a much grander scale. It was important to me to be a consistant presence in their lives. I wanted to make a change that would afford me the flexibility to attend their sports activities and school events. An obvious solution came to me: *become a schoolteacher.* If I could find a job in education, I would have the same hours and vacations the girls had. I didn't waste time thinking about the how's or what ifs. I resigned from my job at Alpha Exports in the early spring of 1998.

I needed a steady income, so I began doing freelance work as a simultaneous interpreter in the Monmouth County Courts system. I also began teaching Spanish to executives and children through two different managing companies, one in Red Bank and one in Princeton. On many occasions I was also called into New York City and other large cities—by corporations like The American Bible

Society, The PGA Tour, and various pharmaceutical companies—to provide interpretation of benefits to Spanish-speaking employees as well as to launch new products. It was fascinating and eclectic work, and I absolutely loved it. I got butterflies in my stomach for each and every assignment, but the work challenged me and ultimately gave me a great sense of ability and accomplishment. I made much more money than I had in New York. Although I worked locally, for the most part, my caseload was unpredictable. Sometimes I had three to four different contracts all over the state in a single day. The work and income were a blessing, but I still urgently needed something that was more aligned with the girls' school schedule. Spending more time with them was imperative, as far as I was concerned. With their father living in Mexico and having limited interaction with them, I was their sole caretaker, support system and cheerleader.

12

Ethics

Late spring, 1998, Monmouth County, New
Jersey, U.S.A.

One of my last assignments as a simultaneous
interpreter took place in the Monmouth
County law offices of a large, well-known firm of
medical malpractice defense attorneys. Their clients
were usually physicians being sued for negligence.
I was to interpret in the deposition of the plaintiff, Jessica, a young, Mexican girl whose son had
been born with severe cerebral palsy, allegedly at the
hands of her doctor's carelessness. It was the type
of work I had done a lot of over the previous couple
of years. I enjoyed it thoroughly, mostly because it

enabled me to help frightened and often hopeless
immigrants who didn't speak or understand English,
to comprehend their legal rights. This gave me a
sense of profound gratification. *Due Process,* whose
roots can be found as far back as The Magna Carta, is
one of the most beautiful components of the United
States Constitution, in my opinion.

By definition, I liked Jessica's lawyer before I
even met him. Plaintiff's attorneys in medical malpractice cases are rooting for the underdog. They
are knights in shining armor, coming to the aid of
those who could conceivably be taken advantage
of, and even perish, if not for them. With this in
mind, it's easy to imagine the profile, personality,
and to a certain extent, the heart of the men and
women who have chosen this type of law to practice. They are almost always compassionate and kind
human beings.

Barry M. Packin, Esq., surpassed my expectations. He was attentive, concerned, and patient with
his client. He had a great sense of humor, albeit
during a serious and tedious process. He even got
Jessica to laugh a few times, through interpretation!
The deposition ended and the defense team and ste-
nographer left the room. For some reason, the three
of us didn't budge. Barry and I sat at the ten-foot
mahogany table, separated by his client, who didn't

seem to mind in the least. We began chatting, as if she wasn't there. He asked me what kind of music I liked, what my hobbies were, a typical conversation that would occur over drinks on a first date. We conversed for a half hour, neither one of us having any apparent time frame or pending commitments. The entire time I thought about how unorthodox, not to mention inappropriate, it would be for me to start a relationship with a professional acquaintance! He gave me his card, but I knew there was no way I would ever call him. I have always had, without exception, a non-negotiable, ethical business code. By the same token, there was nothing I would have enjoyed more. It had been five years since my divorce. I had barely dated since then, and I was ready for a stable and fun relationship. It would take impressive creativity and several months for Mr. Packin to come up with an angle.

13

"KHS"

Autumn, 1998, Keyport, New Jersey, U.S.A.

One mid-September morning, I walked out of the house to my car for something I had forgotten the night before. There, on the ground, was the hefty Sunday edition of the *Star Ledger*, neatly packaged in a blue plastic bag. To this day, I don't know if it was a free promotion or another one of the many small miracles that had occurred during my life. I certainly didn't subscribe to any newspaper. I carried the paper inside and, over my morning coffee, began to peruse the *Classifieds* section. Up until that moment I hadn't started any sort of job search because I simply hadn't had the time. Low and behold, right in the middle of the *Help Wanted* section was an ad for a high school Spanish teacher, in Keyport—only eleven miles away!

I called the next morning and they gave me an appointment for an interview on Friday, September 18th. It must have been an omen, though I didn't notice it at the time. September 18th was my fortieth birthday! My appointment couldn't have gone more smoothly. It turned out that the full-time position was to be shared by two neighboring high schools. In hindsight, it was quite an unusual situation. The principals of both schools simultaneously interviewed and hired me on the spot. There was one glitch: I didn't have a teaching certificate, nor had I taken any education courses in college. Right then, an extraordinary option came to light. The two administrators informed me that, because of the shortage of teachers in the state of New Jersey, a program had been put in place called "the Alternative Route." It provided for eligible candidates to attend night classes over the course of two years to obtain official teacher certification, receiving full salary and benefits in the interim. So, on October 5th, I began what would be a long and fulfilling career in education. As on many other occasions in my life, a solution had emerged exactly when I needed it.

It was as scary as anything I had ever done. I awoke early that Monday morning to get ready for my first day of teaching. It was still dark outside as I sat there in the middle of my bed in a complete panic. My stomach was doing acrobatics as my head simultaneously reeled. Today I would be reporting to, not one, but two different high schools, both of which were located in depressed demographics, unlike anything I had ever experienced. The culture was rough, a bi-product of low education, poverty, and violence. Many of the parents of my students had not graduated from high school, let alone college; nor was it expected or desired. A lot of families had many generations living under the same roof in order to contribute to the household income. In some cases, the kids were encouraged to stay in high school for as long as allowed by law, sometimes up to twenty years old! I imagined my experience would be like a personal version of the 1995 movie with Michele Pfeiffer, *Dangerous Minds*. At the time, I had not yet discovered meditation with its centering and calming effects. I was alone and petrified. In desperation, I turned to the lifelong wisdom Namu had tirelessly shared with me: I began to pray.

My contract stipulated teaching six classes per day, three in each school. Because of the travel time, I would have to eat lunch in the car on the way from

one school to the next, with no prep period or rest. I
had no idea how difficult and unorthodox this was. A
free period is mandatory for all public school teachers
and so is lunch. Furthermore, any classes taught that
exceeded the standard five per day required a sti-
pend by law. Although I did receive the additional,
obligatory money in my paychecks, it did not begin
to offset the added workload. Ignorance, as they say,
is bliss. I had no frame of reference and no expectations. I put my nose to the grindstone and muscled
through the first two grueling years. In those two
years, between the Alternative Route night classes
and daily preparation, I regularly put in eighty-hour
workweeks, trying to keep my head above water. This
being said, I barely noticed how tedious it was. I was
happy and grateful to be working and providing a
stable, predictable life for my little family. Fortunately,
Keyport High School offered me a full-time contract
after my first year, so the challenge of dividing my
time between two schools was short-lived. Plus, as
it turned out, I loved teaching. Despite the six-year
pact I had made with myself to return to interpreting
and translating with easily three times the income, I
continued teaching high school Spanish for thirteen
more years, long after the girls had completed both
high school and college.

Like most things, with time and experience, my job became easier. I served as an inspiration to my students, and they did the same for me. My extroverted and athletic personality enabled me to develop my own, *just-this-side-of-crazy* teaching style. No one ever cut my class. Current Latino, rock and "reggaeton" music filled the air daily as students entered their classroom. No lesson began until I took them into the hall to do a short sequence of yoga poses, designed to stretch their muscles and enhance brain activity. This was, arguably, their favorite part of the day. I was honest and accessible, but had no tolerance for lack of respect. I was kind, fair, and always followed through with consequences for behavioral issues and underperformance. Most of all, the class was fun. My students respected and even loved me, and the feeling was mutual. The symbiotic relationship we established endured year after year. These kids rearranged their schedules, dropped classes, and sometimes failed intentionally in order to get into or stay in my classes. The bottom line was that I taught them more than Spanish, I taught them about life. Subconsciously, it was what they craved. This phenomenon would intensify in later years, when I created an after-school yoga program, open to all students, not only mine. It was successful and popular, as it unexpectedly gave children in a culture that was unstable, depleted, and often dangerous, something invaluable: a tool to manage their stress and anger.

During my first chaotic year at KHS, I remained a stranger to the entire faculty. Since I had no free time, there were no opportunities for bonding with my coworkers. One exception was the French teacher and department head of World Languages. "Coco" and I had a few encounters in the lunchroom, only because she happened to be eating at the same time I raced to make copies. The Xerox machine was in the lunchroom. At times, when I found myself in utter confusion and desperation, I would muster up the courage to ask her for advice. She was a seasoned educator and almost always knew the answers to my questions. Coco had the exceptional and endearing quality of stopping what she was doing to give me her full attention and interest. Even though teachers were only given thirty minutes to gobble down their meals and visit the restroom, she consistently took time and effort to patiently explain the solution to my dilemma du jour.

In addition to possessing more than her share of brains, compassion, and educational experience, Madame Coco was and still is a veritable fashion plate. Truly in keeping with the French culture, she was impeccable, with a chic style toward which anyone would aspire. Not a hair on her head was ever out of place. I was in awe of her "stunning-ness," and, as years passed and our friendship grew, we became each other's fashion mentors. It was a secret joke between the two of us: *The World Language Department single-handedly created and upheld the "standard of style" at KHS!*

Our friendship blossomed into much more than one based on classic clothing trends. To this day we are closer than sisters: *Thelma and Louise, Coco and Frida.* Ours continues to be a remarkable fusion of subdued, confident French elegance and fiery, passionate Latino grace. Both of us are extraordinarily strong and courageous; and we have had to overcome many "would-be" obstacles in our lives. Almost from the beginning, we gradually cultivated a relationship of deep respect, each contributing our unique attributes from opposite sides of the spectrum. After eighteen-plus years, our cherished alliance is alive and well and stronger than ever, despite the thousands of miles that separate us. Thank goodness for Skype!

In a combination of poetic justice and irony, at least for Coco and me, our retirement exodus was one Thelma and Louise would have been proud of. During our time together as coworkers, we often jested that neither of us would survive in the grand institution of KHS without the other. Over the years, the politics in our school district, as well as in the New Jersey Department of Education, had deteriorated beyond recognition. Governor Chris Christie didn't help matters. Policy and procedure became ridiculously lengthy and involved. I think I speak for the majority when I say we felt like circus dogs. It seemed like we had to jump through hoops each time the current concept of education changed in the minds of lawmakers. Every year we were subjected to concepts that were no more efficient, and often more complex and time consuming than the previous ones. This required endless hours of training, testing, and paperwork. It was a pissing match among the powers that be, coupled with a quest to convert all public school educators into a standardized army of clones: predictable, measurable, easy to manage. Creativity, originality, and individuality were eliminated. Everything we did, from lesson plans to student discipline and behavior, stripped us of our singularity, which is what set us apart from computerized online classes. We no longer had the time or the permission to be inventive. The students came last, by sheer virtue of the fact that our clerical workload had more than doubled while the original amount of "prep time" allotted us remained the same. There was literally no time for us to conceive an original, fun curriculum for our students. The

reason we had become teachers had been taken
from us. It was oppressive and frustrating for educators across the state, but most of all, it was a tragedy
for the kids. In mid-June 2013, staying true to our
self-fulfilled prophecy, and conducting our own
personal protest, The World Language Department
proudly walked, practically skipped, arm-in arm out
of the building, never to return. Coco and I did the
right thing by giving timely notice, but the administration would not catch wind of our permanent dis-
appearance until the middle of summer vacation. It
was a healthy dose of virtue rewarded that will surely
keep us entertained for the rest of our lives!

14

The Rock Of Gibralter

October, 1998, Rumson, New Jersey, U.S.A.

My fortieth birthday that year, it turned out, was abundant in the blessings department. Around the time I had been hired by Keyport Regional School District, Barry Packin, Esq., contacted me for professional reasons. Four months had passed and he requested, on behalf of his client and his firm, that I translate, from English to Spanish, the several-thousand-word transcript created from the deposition that had occurred back in May. The purpose for the translation, according to Mr. Packin, was to enable his client, Jessica to read and understand the process she had gone through, helping to

optimally prepare her for the upcoming trial. It was
an ingenious strategy on Mr. Packin's part: I would
be paid for converting a document into the client's
language, and this project would create the necessity
for him and I to collaborate regularly in person. He
had figured out a way to make it appropriate for us
to start a relationship.

The trial of Jessica Padilla, at the time, was
the biggest and most newsworthy medical malpractice case, not only of Barry's career, but in the
state of New Jersey. He and I worked side-by-side
throughout the entire several-month process. As my
function expanded from one of interpreter to the
link between Jessica, her adorable, severely handi-
capped son, José, and anything remotely connected
to the case, I took on an indispensible role in the
trial proceedings. There were doctor appointments,
medical evaluations, interviews with schoolteachers,
even construction estimates for renovations needed
to accommodate José's long-term special needs. The
three of us developed a close friendship over the
months, and they trusted me implicitly. I was their
ally and their connection to the world they lived in,
their sole opportunity to be heard and understood.

Barry and I began dating seriously during
Jessica's trial. We saw each other almost every day,
though Barry kept his apartment in North Jersey.

He would spend the night once or twice during the week, and we spent every weekend together. A factor of considerable strain during our courtship was his ongoing, seriously contentious divorce. Although Barry had been separated and living apart from his wife for two years, they had been married for twenty-two. Barry's children, like their mother, did not want the divorce, even though they were old enough to understand. They were twenty-two and fifteen and had experienced first-hand the daily, sometimes violent, struggles between their parents. Nonetheless, I suppose it's possible they preferred to endure the tense living conditions rather than not having the involvement of their father as a buffer. This did not affect his daughter as much because she was away at college, but both knew their mother well enough to understand that she would not do well without the continuous, intervening guidance and navigation of their father.

The high-stress job description of a medical malpractice litigator together with the arduous, ongoing divorce and the acrimonious posture of Barry's two children toward me, caused what could have been a delightful romance to be one fraught with tension and conflict. After six months of enchanting courtship, and one in which I had become truly invested,

Barry called to tell me it was too much for him. He broke up with me over the phone.

I was blindsided. To this day, I have never had the rug pulled out from under me to such an extent. I had sincerely believed we were on our way toward marriage. The termination of our relationship was completely unexpected. In fact, it destroyed my ability to "trust" for decades, up until recently. In a desperate tactic to anesthetize my pain, I set out on a calculated hunt for a "rebound" fling. In short order I was introduced to a lovely guy, with the perfect combination of "brains and brawn." Having grown up at the Jersey Shore, he was a seasoned surfer who happened to be a mortgage banker. With eyes wide open, I went in for the kill. I needed a distraction in a big way. I didn't know how to handle my emotions so I buried them. At any other time in my life this man could have become my lifetime partner. He was kind, funny, and loved excitement. In the five months we were together we had several bold and thrilling adventures. More than once we took his twenty-three-foot Grady White out to fish for tuna. Since the boat didn't have the fuel capacity for lengthy trips, we would line the cockpit with six full gas cans in order to get out past the sixty-mile mark, where the big fish were. This was highly illegal, not to mention dangerous. We took trips to remote surfing venues in Puerto Rico and the Pacific coast of Mexico. But as action-packed and fun as our time together was, this gentleman never had a chance with me, for no other reason but that I was in love with, and had been devastated by, another man.

Our relationship came to a screeching halt at the wedding of my brother, in September of 2000. I, of course, took my surfer/banker boyfriend as my date, where he met my father and, unbeknownst to me, asked for my hand in marriage. After the celebration he told me the good news. Poor guy. That was the kiss of death. Unfortunately we were at opposing poles in our lives. He was ready to settle down and I had been on a reckless crusade to reassure my ego that I was still desirable. We never saw each other again.

At some point during the wedding I had a heart to heart conversation with my dear friend and confidante, the bride. There wasn't much we didn't share with each other, so she knew what had happened with my previous affair of the heart, and where I was with my current beau. She gave me some great advice with regard to Barry: "If you want him, go and get him. That's what women have to do if we love someone who has gotten away. Men rarely revisit relationships a second time. Women, on the other hand, have the courage to swallow their pride and take a risk. If I hadn't initiated the conversation that eventually led to your brother and I getting back together, we may not have been getting married today."

I gave it a week of thought, but I already knew what I was going to do. I was no stranger to taking risks. My personal case history was actually peppered with them. The following Sunday, bright and early, I called Mr. Packin at home, with every intention of waking him up. I accomplished more than that. Evidently I had also awakened his new girlfriend, with whom he was cohabitating. Like me, he had wasted no time moving forward; however, given the circumstances under which he had ended our relationship, it seemed odd he had been so swift to invite another woman into his life. He later confessed that she had been no more than a warm body, someone to come home to. Nothing serious. It was because of the context of their liason that it ultimately would be dissolved with not too much drama, at least from my perspective. All things considered, he was happy to hear from me. We decided to reconvene at another time for a heartfelt conversation, to which we both looked forward.

The revival of our union was intense and swift. He eliminated his present girlfriend from his home and his life. She too, had been a victim of circumstance, a provisional bandage used to suppress the discomfort of an emotional wound. Within weeks we picked up where we had left off. He broke the lease for his North Jersey apartment and moved into my house in Rumson. It felt good. It was that feeling of gratitude one gets when the rare opportunity for a second chance appears. We both felt lucky. We had almost let each other get away. There was a conscious, mutual appreciation for each other and a willingness to accept things that had previously seemed like deal breakers. In addition, our relationship had taken on a committed and concrete dynamic; we wanted to be married!

The energy in our home felt good. Stefani and Elizabeth liked Barry, and he them. To this day I regard him as an exemplary father, to his biological children, as well as to mine. Almost everything he does, he executes with 100 percent effort. It's in his DNA. It's what makes him an extraordinarily good lawyer as well as an excellent dad. We became a family long before our actual wedding took place. Our lives felt secure and structured, exactly what I had always wanted for my daughters. Everything else was so good that I voluntarily turned a blind eye to our apparent inability to get along harmoniously.

This is a topic that has undergone considerable scrutiny via large amounts of therapy and analysis on both our parts. How can something that is "right" in all other aspects be so difficult and combative at its foundation?

We got married on October 6, 2001, intentionally on Namu's birthday. The next fifteen years had serious ups and downs, but for the most part, we were in it for the long haul. Between Barry's occupation as a successful medical malpractice attorney (at the time he had lost only two cases in his entire career), and mine as a high school Spanish teacher, which included its own valuable perks, we made a good living. We bought a modest house a few blocks from the beach and took regular vacations every year. In the winter, we would go to Palm Beach and in the summer, we'd set aside two weeks in Lake Placid. When the girls were older, we added a special yearly treat: Christmas at the Waldorf Astoria in New York City.

Vacations aside, it was the real-life structure that most bears mentioning. Well before we were married, Barry assumed the role as the girls' father, and he took it seriously. We raised them together, every step of the way. It felt good to have a partner, someone who shared the weight of parenting and marriage equally. There were a few times when Barry's law degree came in handy (speeding tickets, underage drinking, DUIs), but for the most part we were a normal family. "Care Bear," as the girls called him, happily attended countless field hockey and lacrosse games, school plays, and "back to school nights." There were graduations and celebrations, as well as the function of co-disciplinarian during rebellious high school years. When the time came, he helped them move, sometimes to more than one venue, and set up at college. There are too many milestones to count, and he was there for all of them. Generally speaking, the family dynamic was quite good. I now see that we loved each other, but for different reasons. I will be the first to admit that I had never developed a terribly clear or healthy idea of what a loving partnership was. My life experience had been such that I regarded security and stability as the most important components of love. Barry, on the other hand, loved me for me. He loved me romantically, as a wife and partner. I didn't know it at the time, but my subconscious criteria of the foundation of marriage with Barry would not be enough. I began to feel empty and unhappy, but I didn't know why. As time went on it got worse. We became estranged. We had no common interests or things to talk about. It began to wear both of us down. I am quite sure there are many marriages out there that last a lifetime with much less substance than we had. This being said, I believe we both gave our best until there was nothing left. We never lost respect for one another but it eventually became clear that our matrimonial quality of life had disintegrated. We are both warriors with the tenacity to pursue what we want, even if we may not know what that is at the time. No doubt we could have endured the rest of our lives living the way we were, but that would have been like keeping a comatose body on life support indefinitely. Who wants to "endure" their life anyway?

At this moment, I am compelled to momentarily segue, in observation and in reverence to this exceptionally relevant period of my life.

With the assistance of retrospection, I can say with great certainty that the partnership I shared with Barry was one of cosmic importance, for us both. It provided each of us with someone to fall back on, albeit in different capacities. But much more importantly, it gave us a safe, longterm platform on which to mature and learn from each other. We were perfect reflections of one another, though we would have never recognized or admitted it. The personality traits we couldn't abide in the other were directly linked to our own. We were both feisty and headstrong firstborns with a "do or die" necessity to be right ... not a good blueprint for a peaceful relationship. Neither of us had had any example of what normal, successful matrimony looked like, nor had either of us been exposed to a precedent of efficient or respectful squabbling. Barry

*was, and is, a "litigating machine." It's difficult to dis-
cern whether he is an outstanding lawyer because he
has perfected the art of arguing, or, if early on, he had
been drawn to pursue a career in law because of his nat-
ural-born ability to dispute. Regardless, any disagree-
ments between us were an exercise in futility for me. I had
brought my own heavy baggage to the relationship. As
a product of a dysfunctional environment growing up, I
was arrogant and scrappy. My survival mechanism was
to be on the offense, which had been polished and refined
since early adolescence. By definition this was an inevitable equation for great struggle. There is no one to blame.*

Sometimes the biggest blessings come with
the largest price tag. This story cannot be written
without reflecting on my enormous and infinite gratitude to an estimable man. He helped me raise our
children and provided us all with a dignified life,
one with many happy memories and opportunities
that we would not have had without him. He and I
were destined to experience our fifteen-year ven-
ture in order to learn the lessons we were born to
learn. Notwithstanding, we had to end our union in
order to encounter happiness and joy far beyond
that which we had together. Barry Packin, Esq., has
always been and will always be a gentleman and a
true friend in my life.

Something called me. It had called me off and on during my whole life, depending on my level of awareness at any given time. I had never been able to give it a description or a name, but I kept moving toward it. There was a hidden secret to my own purpose and happiness, and it would be discovered when I was ready. On more than one occasion, I can recall family members and friends saying, "I hope you find what you're looking for, Vikki." This was not necessarily delivered as a genuine wish from them to me, rather a reaction to my seemingly unsettled, dissatisfied view of life over many years and three marriages. They viewed me as an irresponsible and temerarious spirit with no plan or direction. I couldn't blame them. If I was unable to identify what was waiting to be unearthed, how could anyone else see where I was heading? It would take courage and conviction for me to follow my inner voice without knowing what was around the corner. All I had was a feeling, but pursuing this feeling had become imperative to my survival. It couldn't be addressed while trapped in a stagnant marriage. I suppose I was ready, because when the unidentifiable mission bubbled to the surface of my consciousness, it was impossible to ignore. The urgency was so paramount to my ongoing existence that I was able to gather the courage it would take to leave my life as I knew it behind.

15

Early Retirement

June 2013, Highlands, New Jersey, U.S.A

About a year and a half before I realized my stint as a public school educator had run its course, I decided to pursue a longtime passion of mine. I decided to sign up for a two hundred-hour course, which would enable me to become certified as a teacher of yoga. I didn't have any plan as to what I would do with this new diploma, but I knew it would unite two true loves of mine: teaching and yoga. As I had done before, I simply followed my gut. No "ends" to the means, just basic spontaneity.

Evenflow Yoga had been my (yoga) home and studio of choice since its inception in 2009. Christian

Valeriani, its owner and founder, was a close, personal friend and my favorite teacher of many years. Realizing such a meaningful accomplishment with him as my instructor was a blessing on many levels. It came at a time when I wasn't sure what I was going to do with my marriage, or the rest of my life. Aside from the obvious practical and theoretical knowledge I gained from this intense program, the spiritual component would become an invaluable tool that would strengthen my chances for surviving the tectonic changes that were right around the corner.

It is said that when we are connected to our true selves, the Universe will conspire to help us. What transpired in my life from that moment on has been a living testament to this philosophy. Every choice I have made, beginning with my yoga certification to the present day, has lined up with astonishing synchronicity. I successfully completed the course in December of 2012 and went on to briefly teach yoga classes at many different studios in Monmouth County. As I mentioned earlier, I also created two after-school yoga programs at Keyport High School, one for students and one for teachers. The overwhelming feeling of fulfillment and gratitude that comes from giving of oneself in service to others is something I had never experienced. It gave me a taste of what I would eventually discover to be the direction my life would take. From the outside I must have looked like the poster child for mid-life crisis.

By early spring of 2013, I began to sense that my teaching career was reaching a dead end. It had been a profession to which I had happily given my heart and soul. It had enabled me to participate fully in my daughters' upbringing and to provide us with wonderful health benefits and the stability of a salary and a pension. I will forever remain grateful for the time I was afforded in this noble vocation. During this period I was inspiring (to) and inspired (by) my students. Their eagerness to learn fueled my passion to teach. I had been in the perfect place at exactly the perfect time. As a teacher, I had been able to express myself fully, in a way that motivated and entertained the kids. It was a win/win scenario that lasted for many years.

Change, as they say, is inevitable. Practically from one day to the next, everything about my job became a struggle. It became tedious instead of fun. Administrative and political obstacles materialized, prompting me to have a serious conversation with myself. "It's time to move on", I concluded. What a blessing. In that moment, I was able to recognize this impetus as a gateway to something new and better even though I had no idea what that "something" was. I began to plan my exit strategy.

It was exciting keeping the secret to myself, well, between Coco and me, for those few months. My intention was to do everything by the book, that is to say, give my sixty-days notice; no more, no less. Therefore, on June 13th, I left the school building just like everyone else, no retirement announcement, no retirement party, and no drama. Around the end of the first week of July, I sent my certified resignation to all the necessary parties and proceeded to savor a most happy and carefree summer. When September came around, I knew it would undoubtedly feel weird to not have to wake up at 6 a.m. or prepare lesson plans for the first time in a decade and a half. It was nothing that would require much getting used to (insert smiley emoticon). What I didn't anticipate was the ensuing responsibility to examine myself and my present life. What did I want? Was I honestly happy and fulfilled? My conclusion was certain: the alternative to maintaining my comfortable, albeit empty, status quo would require a willingness to go to battle. The comfort zone would disappear and I would voluntarily begin a tireless quest to find the truth. It was too much to deliberate at that point. I filed the heart-to-heart conversation with myself to be addressed at another time.

One sunny morning in early December, about six months after I had retired, I sat in my living room. Stefani had just given birth to my first angelic grandchild, and Elizabeth lived in Manhattan, running her own, successful event-planning company. Everyone was in cruise control. I sat in the solitude of the meticulously decorated living room in my lovely home, all which reflected stability. It had been the only thing that mattered at one time. I consciously and cautiously revisited the question I'd asked myself a few months before: Is this all there is? Based on my own, unacceptable conclusions, I made the following decisions, right then and there: *end my marriage, leave Barry the house and all its contents, leave my daughters and brand new granddaughter, sell my car, and move to Mexico.* Just like that, I had unexpectedly made a sweeping declaration to myself. It came with confidence and certitude. This was not all there was! I would pursue the answer with all my heart!

The process leading up to my departure from a life and lifestyle I had co-created with my husband and children was not cut and dried by any stretch of the imagination; nor was it as simple or void of emotion, as it sounds in the preceding paragraph. This was an inevitable decision whose image had rippled just beneath the surface of my awareness for a long time, but I had never had the courage I knew it would require to examine it fully . . . until now. I recognize that my posture probably appeared cold and detached to those on the receiving end of my news. The fact is, it had to be. While I had, and continue to have, tremendous affection, as well as deep compassion for those I left behind, being true to myself was more important. All at once I knew that the definition of love does not include sacrificing one's own happiness. This was it. It was my turn. My focus was on my best interest and no one else's, for the first time in my life. Had I indulged myself in the nostalgia and sadness that surrounded me, I would never have been able to follow through with the stand I had decided to make for myself.

Barry and I had multiple, heartfelt conversations in the weeks that came to pass. They were painful, and yet probably some of the most honest and transparent interactions we had ever had during our fifteen-year marriage. We agreed that we each deserved a relationship with a partner with whom we felt happiness and companionship. There were confessions about the pain of rejection and of not feeling appreciated or admired. We agreed that although we had no idea what was in store for either of us, the decision to "not settle" for a mediocre and lifeless union would eventually bring us something beautiful, even if we ended up alone. Fear of taking the initial step was won over by the logic and the courage it required from both of us to take a leap of faith in the name of our God-given right to live in joy.

Inevitably came a barrage of judgment and emotionally driven conversations, threats, and prophesies, presented mostly by family members. I was unable to blame them. After all, they were only reacting from a place of love and fear. Still, this was the single most difficult stance I had ever taken in my life. Their arguments and opinions were psychologically difficult, almost crippling. Thankfully this forced me to evaluate what I was doing and trust what I felt. It was tremendously empowering, and scary as hell. These adversities ultimately turned out to be important teachers for me.

16

Home Of My Ancestors

March, 2014, Cuernavaca, Morelos, Mexico

In January I began to start lining things up for my journey to a new life in Mexico. One morning I woke up with a vivid idea. My friend Francisca, who had long ago joined the mass exodus from Mexico City, now lived in a sprawling home with terraced grounds at the northern, most elevated part of Cuernavaca, overlooking the city. I knew she had a couple of apartments on her property, which she rented out regularly, sometimes short-term to foreign students or tourists, and sometimes for years at a time to renters who wanted to reside in a "Garden of Eden" environment. I got out of bed and called her immediately. Maybe one of her bungalows was available. Living with her would be like coming home! When I told her I was returning to Mexico to live, she practically jumped through the phone receiver. Yes, one of the smaller cabanas was available, but she wanted to construct an entirely new loft, on one of the lower terraces of the grounds. It would be a private oasis for me, amongst orange trees, with a glass wall that stretched across the entire front of the flat and opened out onto the swimming pool! We quickly reached an agreement. I would arrive in late March. I promptly pre-paid my rent for the year so that she could use the money for the construction of my new home. It was a dream come true, for us both.

As I continued putting one foot in front of the other toward my imminent departure, things just fell into place. The gods were with me and they wanted me to know it. I organized a first-class yoga retreat to Hacienda San Gabriel de las Palmas. In the '70s and '80s it had been one of the private residences of the father of my close friend, Juan Fenton. It had since reincarnated into a five-star boutique hotel with prospects of eventually taking on another incarnation as an international spiritual center. The participants of the retreat were members of my beloved studio: Evenflow Yoga. Hindsight allows me to wax poetic as I rewind the beautiful and gentle unfolding of events that cradled me as I transitioned from one country and one life to another. It was truly a manifestation of love.

The retreat was to begin on March 17th and last for a week. We all met at Newark airport and flew down on the same flight. Private transportation picked us up at the airport in Mexico City, and by late afternoon we were poolside at the Hacienda enjoying an exotic cocktail. I am fairly sure there haven't been many yoga retreats like this one. We had a phenomenal instructor who gave us two classes every day. Melissa Chill, a gifted singer/songwriter and dear friend, had also come on the trip. She accompanied all classes with live music and a voice that would rival that of a love child between Melissa Etheridge and Stevie Nicks. Pure magic. There were three organic and/or vegan meals a day and fresh juices and raw veggies served before afternoon classes.

On March 21st, for the Vernal Equinox, we had an indigenous shamanic guide lead us through a ritual of "rebirth," which began under an unusually enormous full moon. The second half of the ceremony took place inside a Temazcal, a pre-Columbian ritual steam bath that is half physical experience and half spiritual experience. These "sweat lodges" were used by the ancient Mayans as a curative process to purify the mind, body, and spirit. The experience was unforgettable. We finished, stretched out under the stars, covered in warm blankets, drinking sacred herbal tea sweetened with honey.

Our accommodations were palatial suites decorated with impeccably restored period furniture, and we had every amenity one could want. There was a full spa available to us, of which we took full advantage: massages, balancing treatments, aromatherapy, and facials. By the end of the retreat, as I contemplated all the *welcome back, Victoria* experiences, I could admit to myself that none of it had been my imagination. This was where I belonged. This was my home.

The Cuerna Tours bus stopped to drop me off at Francisca's house on the way to the airport in Mexico City. There, the others would take a non-stop flight back to New Jersey. We said our goodbyes, as if we would soon see each other back in the States. I knew that would not happen. It had taken me twenty-four years to get back to the place I had fallen in love with some thirty-six years ago. I wasn't going anywhere.

Francisca met me at the entrance of her house and led me down the meandering rustic steps lined with lush foliage and fragrant, tropical flowers, which brought us to the front door of my newly constructed sanctuary. It was breathtaking. I wept with gratitude.

Miraculous occurrences in my life have been plentiful, attestations to the existence of a higher force, a loving force, a force that wants us to learn and prosper and evolve. I have experienced more inexplicable incidents to name or recount. Countless have looked like luck or coincidence. And then there are those that are beyond reason or explanation when considering my former lifestyle, and frequently audacious choices. The fact that I am currently drawing breath and writing this book is a phenomenon in and of itself. I have tempted fate, even shunned the importance of life, both consciously and, at times, without a second thought. The Universe, God, whatever you choose to call it, has intervened. I had something powerful and good to accomplish in my life, therefore I needed to stay alive to make that happen. We've all heard the expression, "when the student is ready, the teacher will appear." I am living proof of the validity of this saying. I will also tell you, that try as you may, the journey cannot be accelerated.

The development, unfolding, and execution of the process that brought me back to my beloved Mexico is one I count among my most fortuitous episodes. In this instance I speak of the teachers. They have appeared in succession, one after another for me, in ways and in places that could not have been planned or foreseen.

I had been living in Mexico for about six months when Francisca left the country for a month-long trip. She had rented one of the apartments on the property and left me in charge of the tenant and any questions or problems that could have arisen.

Androna had arrived during the day while I was out. It was fairly late when I got home, but I headed up the corkscrew staircase that led to the apartment to quickly introduce myself. Before I had gotten halfway up, an adorable puppy, a little like a Pomeranian, came bounding down the steps. Her owner, who was chit-chatting with in the dog in flawless English, closely followed. We bumped into each other and introduced ourselves in Spanish, which was normal since she is Mexican and thought I was too. I began laughing hysterically at what I had just witnessed: a Hispanic woman speaking fluent English (with no accent) to her dog! In an instant we were talking as if we had known each other for years. It was late so we decided to continue our tête-à-tête in the morning over coffee.

The next day was more of the same: a non-stop dialogue between two strangers who had made an instant connection. After more than two hours I had to leave for a BBQ with friends. I wouldn't see Androna again before she left so we bid each other farewell and exchanged contact information. She also mentioned she would be attending a nine-day seminar in Mexico City in a few weeks that she thought I might enjoy. She would later send me some YouTube links to videos of the same people who would give the approaching seminar, so I could see if I was interested.

The videos were of classes given by Maha Vajra and Shivagam (Maha Vajra's lifetime student). Both are internationally revered spiritual masters whose teachings are rooted in Buddhism yet encompass all traditions. Their instruction was immediately understandable and made sense. This was exactly the kind of tutelage I had been looking for, for many years! I decided to attend both weekends of the upcoming seminar Androna had suggested to me.

I had never attended this type of event and I was a bit nervous. I devoured the seventeen-plus videos Androna recommended I watch, which made me feel more comfortable and familiar with the material. I was excited. I knew this was going to be big for me.

Androna met me at the event. She knew everyone, not the least of whom were Maha and Shivagam, themselves. The workshop was Maha's, and because he is Canadian and speaks French and English, Shivagam served as his simultaneous interpreter.

I was introduced to everyone. I have never met such warm, sincere people, including the two masters. I suppose, that at some point during the first weekend, Maha had instructed Androna to be my teacher. I was overjoyed. Finally I had someone to guide me. And so my odyssey commenced. Step by step, with Androna's careful supervision, I began to follow the teachings set forth in the Mahajrya, the teachings of Maha Vajra and Shivagam. I will be perpetually thankful for the privilege of knowing Androna. She was the angel specifically sent to me that set my life-changing course in motion.

I can now affirm with complete certainty that my life may be measured in two halves: My life before meeting these two Masters, and all that has followed.

Some time has passed since that defining moment, forever etched in my mind's eye. Life continues to align itself for me, without much ado. I remember I had some distinct ideas of what I would do when I first got here to Mexico and what my life would look like. In short order I discovered that few of my preconceived notions would materialize. Interestingly, it didn't matter. I began to let go. Little by little I accepted that everything would happen exactly the way it was supposed to. Hadn't it been that way all along? Hadn't everything fallen into place without my help? Simply allowing things to unfold and trusting the process of life has been the most powerful lesson I have ever experienced.

There is no denying that I do my part. I wake up every day and put forth all the effort and passion I possess. And guess what? It's a pleasure. I certainly won't say it's easy, but at least it seems that way when considering the alternative, which is continued suffering. Namu used to say to me, "When you are doing what's right for you, everything lines up."

I continue to be deeply involved in my spiritual studies and dedicated to my process. I am more disciplined and healthy, both mentally and physically, than I have ever been in my entire adult life. The most important realization however, came to me not too long ago, on my fifty-seventh birthday: I have never felt this complete, fulfilled, and truly happy—ever. This is what had been tugging at me for all those years. I knew there was something else. I felt it. There had been an enormous void in my life, and it took many years, many setbacks, and ultimately dauntless perseverance to identify its origin. Make no mistake: this thing called "life" is a continuous excursion for us all. It is jam-packed with experiences, twists and turns all designed to help us master ourselves . . . to give us the opportunity to develop our own personal, intimate relationship. Nonetheless, it is a treasure, often hidden in plain sight. It is a prize available to us all, but not always easy to attain. After all this time, I have unearthed from the depths within myself, the path that leads to *the philosopher's stone*, which for so long was outside of my field of vision. It has been a beautiful pilgrimage, so far, and one that is without end, but along the way I have found the gift of getting to know myself.

Epilogue

J uan Pablo Flores Guerrero came into my life as he had come into this world, with assertive yet unintentional and charming determination. His mother, Silvia, who has become a dear friend, tells the story of his birth: "He was conceived when his brother was only two months old and I was on birth control pills!" Then there was a long struggle after he was born to stabilize some serious health issues.

The onset of our union was just as fateful. By all accounts, "being in a relationship" was out of the question. Neither of us was looking for romance, especially me. My life was complicated enough. Now that I was in Mexico, I yearned for solitude and time to get to know myself. I needed a long rest. Once again, the Universe had other plans, and I will be endlessly grateful that it did.

I reached my new home on Sunday, March 24th, when the shuttle bus transporting the participants of the yoga retreat to the airport, deposited me at my front door. That same evening, Francisca had organized a small get-together in celebration of my arrival. Among the guests was the gentleman who had been in charge of the design and construction of my new apartment, Juan Pablo. He was a close, personal friend of Francisca's, and she thought it would be nice for us to meet.

The evening was perfect: fascinating people from different parts of the world, heavenly weather, Cole Porter crooning in the background, delicious wine, and exotic hors d'oeuvres. There was engaging conversation and dancing followed by dinner al fresco on a sweeping terrace overlooking the entire city of Cuernavaca. Because the neighborhood is located high above the main city, there are no street or commercial lights to compete with the celestial show that occurs at nightfall. The sky transitioned into ink-blue velvet as stars and constellations began to take their places, filling the canvas above us with jeweled splendor. It was spellbinding.

At around midnight, the guests began to bid goodnight, as did Francisca. JP and I stayed out under the stars and talked until daybreak. I hadn't done that since my twenties! We ran into each other again, later on that week, at which time I made my second feeble attempt to convince him that we had no business getting involved. He agreed.

After we had seen each other several more times in the next two weeks it became obvious that neither of us was kidding anyone. The attraction was irresistible. We loved each other's company and spent hours and hours in deep conversation, plus he made me laugh! For the first time in my life I decided to stop analyzing the situation and just flow with it. What was the worst that could happen?

At the time, Silvia, JP's mother, had been recovering from surgery, and he had moved into her house to take care of her. By the end of April, I too had migrated over to her house. The fact that I had a brand new, gorgeous pad across town that had been paid in advance for the entire upcoming year was utterly unimportant to me at that moment. It just didn't matter. We craved more time together and this was a (temporary) solution. Silvia, it turned out, is an enchanting, intelligent, and fun woman (I can see where her son gets it). She looks and acts two decades younger than she is. I adored the time I spent in her home getting to know her. We did yoga and meditated together regularly. We shared war stories and food recipes. It was delightful.

Days turned into months and the months have now become years. JP and I have long since left

Silvia's home and live in our own idyllic three-bed-room penthouse in the center of Cuernavaca. We still spend the better part of every single day together. We share an office and sit for hours at our computers, touching our feet together under the massive wood desk. Because I'm an early riser, I shoot for going to sleep no later than 10 p.m. each night, but my feeble attempt at discipline continues to be sabotaged regularly. Most nights I fall asleep closer to midnight. We haven't tired of our companionship in the least. There's a good hour or more of nocturnal conversation each night when the lights go out.

Far beyond the friendship and conviviality, what JP and I share is something much more essential. It is the foundation upon which the possibility to exist in joy and peace rests. Juan Pablo is a simple and happy soul, "having a human experience," as they say. He has no agenda and few expectations. He wakes up each day with a broad and genuine smile, an archetype for anyone in his midst. He has truly led me by his own example. The man is thrilled to be alive. He is tickled to death to be with me, just the way I am to be with him. He is delighted to be living *today*, and gives none of his energy toward concern for the longterm. There is a lightness that comes when the burden of control begins to dissolve. His unconscious illustration of this has inspired me to want to be the best person I can be, and to begin to release my own, deeply rooted compulsion to control everything.

Silvia tells people I am an angel that fell from the sky and landed in the middle of their close-knit family. My thoughts on the subject are a bit different: Juan Pablo claimed his right to be born, against all odds, and continued living his (less than easy) life with the same conviction. He waited . . . waited for something he was unable to identify but knew was important. And that was enough. Juan Pablo was born to cross my path, and I his.

My life has become a testament to the power and enormity of faith. Listen to your inner voice. Don't settle for a life that doesn't feel right. Even if you can't see the big picture right away, even if you're scared to death. Take responsibility for creating what you want for yourself, complete responsibility. And then, take hold of the opportunity for an existence that surpasses your wildest dreams!

About the Author

Victoria Takács was born in Wilmington, Delaware, where she attended Wilmington Friends School from kindergarten through tenth grade. After high school, and a brief attempt at college, she took a two-week vacation to Mexico, from which she did not return for twelve years. The story of her life has been one with many inspirational twists and turns, thus insisting on being told. Victoria is a writer, former high school Spanish teacher, and certified yoga instructor. She holds a degree in Spanish, specializing in simultaneous interpretation and literary translation. She currently resides in Cuernavaca, Mexico, where she teaches meditation and yoga.

CPSIA information can be obtained
at www.ICGtesting.com
Printed in the USA
BVOW08s1038160817
492219BV00001B/1/P